INDEPENDENT CONSULTING

The Definitive Guide

(Revised edition)

Elijah M. James, Ph. D.

Canadian Cataloguing in Publication Data

James, Elijah M.

Independent Consulting: The Definitive Guide

ISBN 978-1-998692-00-2

EJ Publishing
663 White Plains Run
Hammonds Plain
Nova Scotia, Canada   B4B 1W7

This book is dedicated to the memory of my beloved Aunt, the late Ida Simon (Goddie), who exemplified patience, resilience, and confidence—the very qualities that define an exceptional independent consultant. Her wisdom continues to inspire my journey and this work.

Table of Contents

PREFACE

When I wrote *Independent Consulting: The Definitive Guide*, over 20 years ago, I indicated that the main reason for writing the book was to help consultants and other professionals run successful practices. This edition has a similar objective. Whether you are a veteran consultant or contemplating entering the field, this book is a definitive guide.

Independent Consulting: The Definitive Guide is neither a manual on consulting exclusively nor a textbook on consulting exclusively. Instead, it is a combination of both. If you are interested in consulting as an accountant, the book does not provide you with the necessary accounting skills. It assumes that you are already appropriately qualified as an accountant. However, it does provide the consulting skills that will help to make you a successful independent consultant in accounting.

Independent Consulting is designed for a wide readership. It will appeal specifically to the following:

- independent consultants in any field

- professionals and others who are contemplating entering the consulting field

- students in colleges and universities that offer a course in consulting

- people and organizations that use the services of consultants.

The book will also serve as a useful reference for a variety of topics. Whether you are a seasoned independent consultant, a rookie, or a prospective independent consultant, you will find this book to be quite useful in many ways.

Special Features

1. *Independent Consulting: The Definitive Guide* is written in plain English. Technical jargon is used only where it is necessary.

2. The book combines textbook features with a "manual" approach to produce a good balance of theory and practice.

3. Significant amounts of illustrations are used throughout the book.

4. The author shares his considerable experiences as an independent consultant with the readers as a means of illustrating certain points, with the hope that such experiences will influence decisions that independent consultants will have to make.

5. Each chapter introduces the reader to the material that will be covered in the chapter.

6. The summary at the end of each chapter serves as a quick review of the material presented in the chapter.

7. Each chapter contains an objective "self-test" so that readers can assess their comprehension and level of mastery of the material. Answers are provided at the end of each test set.

The book is conveniently divided into 14 chapters, covering the bare facts you need to know to run a successful consulting business. Chapters 1 and 2 introduce readers to independent consulting and the consulting business. Chapters 3, 4, and 5 cover various aspects of marketing as they relate to the consulting business. Chapter 3 begins the discussion on marketing consulting services. Chapter 4 continues the discussion, examining certain marketing methods. Chapter 5 deals with the all-important marketing plan. The fee that consultants charge for their services determines their income. That is the subject of Chapter 6. Chapter 7 discusses proposal writing while Chapter 8 examines report writing. The consulting interview is the focus of Chapter 9 while Chapter 10 concerns itself with planning and controlling assignments. Chapters 11 and 12 discuss managing a consulting business and consulting contracts respectively. Chapters 13 and 14 end the book with a discussion of independent consulting and artificial intelligence (AI) and the future of independent consulting respectively.

The dish has been prepared. The table is set. Help yourself to a hefty serving of *Independent Consulting: The Definitive Guide*. Bon appetit!!

INDEPENDENT CONSULTING

ACKNOWLEDGEMENTS

I have incurred an unusually large debt in the course of writing this book. Several people have given me a great deal of their time, energy, advice, suggestions, and encouragement, and have contributed in many other ways to making this book a reality. I must express my gratitude to them.

First, I must thank my son, Dr. Ted James, who planted the idea of this book in my head. In one of our conversations, he asked, "Why don't you write a book on the essentials of independent consulting?" I thought about it and decided that I would. Thanks, Ted.

I owe a comparable debt to my daughter, Andrea who *demanded* (she thinks she has the right to do that) to know what I was doing in my office on a Sunday that was my birthday. When I explained the project to her, she declared that it was "cool." Andrea, thanks for your consistent encouragement and support.

I am also indebted to my students in my MBA classes at Concordia University, Montreal. Repeatedly they asked questions about various aspects of the independent consulting process. Their questions directed my attention to the more significant issues in independent consulting. The selection of topics for inclusion in this book was directed, in part, by those questions.

Koren Norton has once more demonstrated her unselfishness by sacrificing that valuable resource that we call time, which is scarce for the vast majority of us, but which was particularly scarce for her while I was preparing the manuscript. She took time from her busy schedule to attend to my needs so that I could focus on writing the book. I owe her a tremendous debt of gratitude. Thanks, Koren, you are terrific.

I must also thank my dear friend, Veronica Martin-Batson, for constantly reminding me of the words of the wise man Solomon who said, "...I perceive that there is nothing better, than that a man should rejoice in his own works..." Veronica, thanks for the inspiration.

Finally, I must thank my Aunt, the late Ida Simon (Goddie), who, by precept and example, has taught me the art of problem-solving. As an independent consultant, I have had the opportunity to apply her teaching to many of my clients' problems. I do not have words enough to express my gratitude to her.

Elijah M. James

CHAPTER 1
INTRODUCTION TO
CONSULTING

INTRODUCTION

Independent consulting is an exciting field of work. Like other areas of business, it has its advantages and disadvantages. Those of us who have become and remained independent consultants believe that the benefits (advantages) outweigh the costs (disadvantages). This introductory chapter explores the nature of independent consulting. It touches on a variety of issues relating to independent consulting and lays the groundwork for further discussions in later chapters.

WHAT IS INDEPENDENT CONSULTING?

A definition of consulting seems to be a good place to start. For purposes of this discussion, we define consulting as the process whereby independent and knowledgeable people provide expertise to others for a fee. There are at least four points worth noticing in this definition:

1. Consulting is a process
2. Consultants are independent
3. Consultants are experts
4. Consultants are paid for their expertise.

Let us examine each of these assertions:

Consulting as a Process

A process implies a series of steps. A typical consulting engagement ends with the consultant providing the client with expert advice to enable the client to make a decision that will solve a particular problem. The consultant does not make the decision (that's the client's job) unless he/she is asked to do so, but he/she facilitates good decision-making. In order to arrive at the juncture where expert advice can be given, the consultant must go through the following steps outlined in Figure 1.1.

Step 1. Identify the Problem

The first step in the consulting process is to identify the problem. Before the consultant can assist his/her client in making a decision (solving a problem), he/she must first understand and define the problem. Care must be taken to identify the real problem rather than the symptoms.

```
┌─────────────────────────┐
│     IDENTIFY THE        │
│       PROBLEM           │
└─────────────────────────┘
            ↓
┌─────────────────────────┐
│        GATHER           │
│      INFORMATION        │
└─────────────────────────┘
            ↓
┌─────────────────────────┐
│       EXAMINE           │
│     ALTERNATIVES        │
└─────────────────────────┘
            ↓
┌─────────────────────────┐
│     SELECT BEST         │
│     ALTERNATIVE         │
└─────────────────────────┘
            ↓
┌─────────────────────────┐
│      RECOMMEND          │
│      SOLUTION           │
└─────────────────────────┘
            ↓
┌─────────────────────────┐
│   GATHER FEEDBACK,      │
│   EVALUATE RESULTS      │
└─────────────────────────┘
```

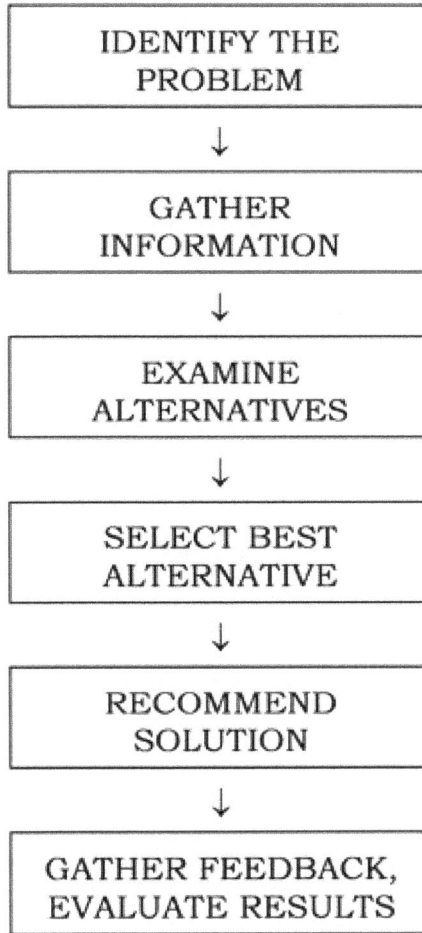

Figure 1.1. The Consulting Process

For example, a manager may observe a high job turnover, what could be the real cause? Perhaps one of the first things that will come to mind is inadequate wages and salaries. But this might not be the case at all. Perhaps the real cause is a lack of recognition and appreciation of the efforts of employees by management.

Let's consider another example. It has just rained, and water is flowing from a particular spot in the ceiling.

Certainly, there is a leak; but the leak may be located several meters from the immediate vicinity of the flow. These two examples illustrate the need for serious investigation in order to diagnose the problem.

The *5 Whys* technique helps identify the problem. Let us assume that a manufacturing company is experiencing frequent delays in product delivery. A consultant is called in to identify the cause of the problem. To do so, the consultant asks the 5 whys as follows:

1. **Why are the products being delivered late?**
   Answer: Because production is taking longer than expected.

2. **Why is production taking longer than expected?**
   Answer: Because one of the assembly machines frequently breaks down.

3. **Why does the assembly machine frequently break down?**
   Answer: Because it hasn't been maintained regularly.

4. **Why hasn't it been maintained regularly?**
   Answer: Because there is no preventive maintenance schedule in place.

5. **Why is there no preventive maintenance schedule in place?**
   Answer: Because management prioritized cost-saving over maintenance planning.

Root Cause Identified:

The lack of a preventive maintenance schedule is the root cause of the delays.

Step 2. Gather Information

Once the problem has been correctly identified, the next step in the process is to collect relevant information. This step is extremely important because problems do not exist in a vacuum. Here is where the consultant's training, experience, and expertise will prove to be of utmost benefit. Relevant information might include current and expected interest rates, the age of equipment components, symptoms displayed, previous attempts made to correct the problem, etc.

Step 3. Examine or Develop Alternatives

Many problems do have a unique solution. For example, a damaged part may have to be replaced. In most cases, however, there are alternative solutions. If the alternatives are obvious, the consultant needs to examine them carefully. If they are not so obvious, then the consultant needs to generate alternatives. Consulting involves choosing the optimal solution from the list of feasible solutions.

Step 4. Select the Best Alternative

Once the alternatives have been listed and examined, the next step in the consulting process is to select the most beneficial alternative. On the basis of criteria derived from the client's objective(s), alternatives must be evaluated and a recommendation made.

Step 5. Make Recommendations

Unless the consultant is engaged to make decisions for the client, his/her role is to *recommend*. Often, this is easier said than done. The analysis and interpretation of the problem may create difficulties for a clear-cut recommendation. The recommendation may be a tough one, which, if implemented, may affect many people adversely. Just as managers are often faced with tough decisions, so too consultants are often obliged to make tough recommendations. The consultant may also be asked to help to implement the recommendations.

Step 6. Gather Feedback and Evaluate the Results

Except for particular cases, the consultant's job does not end with making the recommendations. The results of the recommendations, if implemented, must be evaluated. This is done by gathering feedback to determine the effect of the decision. The feedback may be in the form of a simple telephone call to the client to determine whether the problem has been solved satisfactorily, or it may be in the form of another visit by the "patient" (the client) so that the physician (the consultant) can determine the effect of the treatment administered. If the chosen recommendation fails to solve the problem, then the consultant must search for alternative solutions.

Consultants are Independent

The term "independence" implies freedom from the control, authority or influence of others. Independent consultants are not *employees* of their clients.

Certainly, without clients using the services of consultants, there would be no independent consultants. However, the award of a contract or an engagement does not confer employee status on independent consultants. Clients do not *control* the consultants' income, their working hours, their place of work, or other aspects of their working conditions. Independent consultants are masters of their own destinies.

It must be noted, however, that this independence does not imply that consultants have direct authority over changes to be made as a result of their recommendations. Of course, it is the responsibility of independent consultants to involve their clients in the consulting process, so that the probability of implementation and ultimate success will be maximized.

Consultants as Experts

An expert may be defined as one whose knowledge or skill is specialized and profound as a result of study and experience. Only experts can be expected to provide expertise on a continuing basis. Consultants enter the consulting business because they believe they possess some specialized knowledge for which clients are willing to pay. The expertise may be obtained from years of study or practical experience, and it may be acquired in any field. For example, a medical doctor may specialize in orthopedic surgery and become a consultant in that field, or an auto mechanic may specialize in auto electrical systems and become a consultant in that field.

Consultants are Paid

Our definition of consulting suggests that consultants are paid for their expert advice. Many knowledgeable people offer their services voluntarily, for free. Although their contribution may be laudable, they are not considered consultants in the sense in which we use the term. They may be philanthropists, but they are not consultants. This does not suggest that independent consultants do not do anything for which they are not paid. It does suggest, however, that when independent consultants give advice in their professional capacity as consultants, they should be paid.

WHY PEOPLE BECOME INDEPENDENT CONSULTANTS

Independent consultants are consultants who have the freedom to decide what they will do and when they will do it. They decide whether or not they will work for a certain client, and they decide how much they will charge for their services. They decide whether they will work on an assignment during the early hours of the morning or late in the afternoon. They are their own bosses.

Independent consultants may work at home, in offices by themselves, or with other employees, or they may be engaged by consulting firms to work on certain assignments. Their distinguishing mark is that their success does not depend directly on decisions made by others. Certainly, a prospective client can decide not to engage the services of a particular consultant, in the same way that a firm can decide not to hire a Human

Resources Officer. However, once engaged, the independent consultant enjoys a freedom, an independence, that an employee does not experience.

An example will illustrate the difference between an employee and an independent consultant. An accountant employed by a corporation usually has predetermined hours of work (even though the so-called "flex time" is changing that fact), a set salary, and normally does not have the opportunity to choose his/her clients. That accountant's success may be directly dependent upon decisions made, not by him/her, but by the executives of the company. He/she is not independent. If that same accountant were an independent consultant engaged by the company, he/she would be paid for his/her services, and his/her success as a consultant would be independent of the executives' decisions.

The Varieties of Consultants

Consulting is multi-dimensional. If it is possible to become an expert in a particular field, then it is also possible to become an independent consultant in that field. Here is a short list of consulting fields, just to give you an idea of the breadth of the consulting business.

- Acoustical consultants
- Advertising consultants
- Agricultural consultants
- Art consultants
- Audio visual consultants
- Automotive consultants
- Aviation consultants

- Bankruptcy consultants
- Breastfeeding consultants
- Bridal consultants
- Broadcast consultants
- Building consultants
- Business consultants
- Carpet consultants
- Colour & style consultants
- Combustion & heating consultants
- Communication & Public Relations consultants
- Computer consultants
- Construction management consultants
- Educational consultants
- Electronic consultants
- Elevator consultants
- Energy consultants
- Estate planning consultants
- Executive search consultants
- Fashion consultants
- Freight traffic consultants
- Fund raising consultants
- Government relation consultants
- Hotel & motel consultants
- Industrial relations consultants
- Insolvency consultants
- Laboratory consultants
- Labour relations consultants
- Loss prevention consultants

- Management consultants
- Marketing consultants
- Mining consultants
- Motion picture consultants
- Nutrition consultants
- Quality control consultants
- Real estate consultants
- Roofing consultants
- Safety consultants
- Space planning consultants
- Sports consultants
- Tax consultants
- Telecommunications consultants
- Telemarketing consultants
- Welding consultants

Some categories within the consulting field may overlap. For example, a chartered accountant may be a financial consultant, a tax consultant, and a business consultant. Moreover, there may be sub-specialties within categories. For example, one medical consultant may specialize in oncology, while another may specialize in obstetrics.

Internal and External Consultants

Consultants may also be classified as internal or external consultants. *Internal* consultants typically work within an organizational setting. They are employed within particular organizations such as private utility companies, or government agencies or departments. Their services are usually provided exclusively to the organization by which they are hired. Their main function is to provide expert advice and specialized services to the organizations that hire them. They are not independent consultants as we have defined the term.

External consultants are totally independent of the organizations or individuals who use their services. Particular assignments may cause external consultants to perform some of their work within the organizations that engage their services. However, unlike their internal counterparts, they leave the organizations once their assignments are finished. Since we are concerned mainly with independent consulting, the greater part of our discussion will relate primarily to external consultants.

Reasons for Becoming Independent Consultants

People become independent consultants for different reasons, but for most independent consultants, the most important reason can be translated into one word, **independence**. The motivating force behind the desire to become an independent consultant is the desire to be one's own boss the desire to be independent. If you would really prefer to work for someone else, then you should forget about independent consulting and try to find work as an employee.

Some consultants earn a great deal of money, and it would be naive to think that no one has ever been lured into consulting by the money that can be made. But for many, the "bottom line" is not the determining factor. Other reasons that motivate people to become independent consultants include:

- the possession of marketable specialized knowledge, skills, and experience
- the necessity of earning a living
- the expectation of extra income
- the prestige associated with consulting.

We shall discuss each of these motives in turn.

Marketable Skills and Experience

Your expertise in a particular area might provide strong motivation to enter the consulting business. Perhaps you have worked for many years as a teacher, a school principal, a school superintendent, and as chairman of a school board. You are an acknowledged expert in the area of elementary and secondary education.

You have established that there is a demand for consulting services in this field, and you have identified your target market as mainly school boards and parents with children of elementary and secondary school age. Under these circumstances, you may consider entering the consulting business as an educational consultant.

The Necessity of Earning a Living

No matter how talented or experienced you are, it is possible to become unemployed. The tendency of firms to downsize and to engage in "outsourcing" has rendered employment less permanent for any employee. Several years ago, a job today meant a job tomorrow. Today, a job today means a job today. Except for a select few, earning a living means having a job.

The threat of unemployment with its concomitant loss of income is a strong motivating force in the decision to become an independent consultant. Most people would consider it a necessity to earn a living. As an employee, economic conditions may prevent you from earning a living. As an independent consultant, you have greater control over when you work and how much you work. Consulting is a good way to earn a living.

The foregoing in no way implies that income is automatic once you have become an independent consultant. There are many examples of people who jump into the consulting arena without the necessary tools. Merely being good at something does not guarantee success as an independent consultant. Market conditions, the state of the industry, pricing, management and organization, and other variables all play important roles in determining the consultant's success.

The Expectation of Extra Income

Most people can do well with a little extra income. The desire to earn extra income has motivated some people to become consultants. The flexibility of consulting hours makes this prospect rather appealing. If you have extra time on your hands after your full-time job, such as evenings and weekends, and if you are an expert in some field, you can earn extra income by getting into consulting on a part-time basis. This is exactly how many consultants enter the consulting business.

If you are a retiree with lots of experience and knowledge in some field, you might consider setting up a small office at home and offering your services to friends, previous employers, and other acquaintances.

The Prestige Associated with Consulting

Consulting is seen as a prestigious and glamorous business that may be appealing to many. Consulting may bring you into contact with top business executives, government officials, great educators, and all kinds of interesting people. Being an independent consultant may allow you to rub shoulders with the cream of society, so to speak. If you like to fly, independent consulting allows you to travel across international boundaries several times a year at your choice. It can be a glamorous job, but somebody has to do it. That somebody can be you.

QUALITIES REQUIRED FOR SUCCESSFUL INDEPENDENT CONSULTING

You may have excellent reasons for becoming (or wanting to become) an independent consultant, but the reasons are not enough to make you a successful independent consultant. Successful independent consultants have certain abilities, and there are actual tests that you can take to help you decide whether you have the qualities to be a successful independent consultant. (No one has yet designed a perfect test for this purpose).

Among the characteristics that successful independent consultants possess are the following:

- love of independence and freedom
- expertise in one or more areas
- the ability to command respect and trust

- "sticktoitability" (stick to it ability): the ability to complete projects even in the face of severe obstacles
- the ability to handle responsibility
- the ability to persuade people
- creativity and initiative
- the ability to analyze a situation or problem and find a solution
- confidence in their knowledge and abilities
- the ability to handle success.

You may feel that you do not possess many of these qualities to any significant degree. Don't despair. Many independent consultants succeed on the strength of their love of independence, their expertise, and their *desire* to be successful.

The Independent Consultant's Formal Education

A very frequently asked question is, "Do I need a degree to be an independent consultant"? The answer is no. A degree from a college or university is evidence that you have acquired a certain amount of *academic* information. Certainly, a degree (especially an advanced degree) will help you as a consultant because it does provide added credibility. But your value as a consultant depends crucially on your expertise which is derived largely from your special talent and experience.

Lack of a high level of formal education is not a barrier to becoming a successful independent consultant. Many areas of consulting do indeed require a substantial amount of formal education. For example, an economic consultant without graduate-level training in economics would probably have a difficult time obtaining clients, and a legal consultant without substantial formal training in law might encounter more than just a credibility problem.

However, many areas of consulting do not require any high level of formal education. Expertise can be acquired through experience. For example, a materials handler consultant may not even be exposed to higher education. (How many colleges and universities offer degrees in materials handling?) But years of experience and special talent may contribute to an individual's expertise in that area, and cause him/her to become a successful independent consultant.

WHERE CONSULTANTS WORK AND WHAT THEY DO

If you are already in the consulting business, you know where you work and what you do. If you are planning to enter the consulting field, you probably have some ideas about what you would like to do and where you would like to work. However, you are only one of myriads of consultants. Refer to our truncated list of types of consultants mentioned earlier in the chapter.

In part, where consultants work is a function of the type of consulting that they do. A roofing consultant must often visit buildings, a business consultant will likely visit the client's business location, and an advertising consultant may be able to work substantially from his/her home or office.

Although an independent consultant may need to spend a great deal of time at his/her client's workplace or the client's home, the vast majority of independent consultants spend some amount of time working at home or in their offices.

Consultants can be found working:

- in private firms such as large manufacturing establishments, airline companies, and small business enterprises

- in research institutions, giving advice in their area of expertise

- in courts as expert witnesses

- in governmental organizations advising government officials and agents

- in hospitals as administrative consultants or as medical consultants

- in not-for-profit organizations as advisers

- in international organizations as experts in certain fields.

In short, consultants can be found *everywhere*.

What consultants do also depends on the type of consultant. A financial consultant and a plumbing consultant obviously do quite different things. Even consultants in the same general field may do quite different things. For example, one management consultant may specialize in organizational effectiveness and efficiency (such a consultant is often referred to as an efficiency expert), while another may specialize in human resources management and salary administration.

Detailed descriptions of what every consultant does would constitute an entire book. A partial list of the main activities of the more popular consulting categories follows, and where the consultants offering those services are likely to work. In order to provide a sense of the varieties of consulting functions, we include in our short list, consulting services to both private and business clients. For convenience, the list is arranged alphabetically.

Advertising Consultants

Advertising consultants:

- assess the characteristics of products and services to be promoted and advise on the advertising needs of clients

- advise clients on advertising or sales promotion strategies

- develop and implement or assist with the implementation of advertising campaigns, advising on the appropriate media to be used.

These consultants are engaged by management consulting firms, advertising agencies, and throughout the public and private sectors.

Agricultural Consultants

Agricultural consultants:

- provide counseling and advisory services to farmers on crop cultivation and fertilization, harvesting, animal and poultry care, disease prevention, farm management, farm financing, marketing, and other agricultural subjects

- prepare and conduct advisory information sessions and lectures for farmers and other groups
- conduct research, analyze agricultural data and prepare research reports
- study agricultural policies and advise governments and other groups on their impact.

Agricultural consultants offer their services mainly to businesses, institutions, and governments that assist the farming community.

Bridal/Wedding Consultants

Bridal consultants advise clients on:

- the selection of wedding gowns
- floral arrangements
- banquet facilities
- wedding invitations
- other items related to weddings

Bridal/Wedding consultants are engaged mainly by fashion schools, wedding consulting firms, and the general public.

Business/Management Consultants

Business and management consultants:

- analyze and provide advice on management and organizational methods and procedures in private and public establishments,

- and conduct research to determine the efficiency and effectiveness of managerial policies and programs

- propose improvements to methods, systems, and procedures in areas such as operations, human resources, and communications

These consultants are engaged mainly by management consulting firms, business establishments, service organizations, advertising agencies, and throughout the public and private sectors.

Colour/Fashion Consultant

Colour consultants advise clients on the choice of colours for clothing that will complement their appearance. Fashion consultants advise on hairstyle, make-up, clothing and accessories in order to improve personal and business image and appearance.

Colour and fashion consultants are engaged mainly by beauty salons, fashion boutiques, and modeling schools.

Communications & Public Relations Consultants

Consultants in this category:

- develop and evaluate communications strategies and programs designed to inform clients, employees, and the general public of initiatives and policies or businesses, governments and other organizations

- assist with the implementation of communications strategies and programs
- prepare reports, briefs, speeches, presentations and press releases for clients
- develop and organize workshops, meetings, ceremonies, and other events for publicity, fundraising and information purposes
- initiate and maintain contact with the media

Consultants in this category offer their services mainly to consulting firms, corporations, associations, governments, social agencies, and other organizations.

Computer Consultants

Computer consultants:

- confer with clients regarding the nature of the information processing or computation needs a computer program is to address
- analyze these needs into related components which can be solved through the application of computer technology
- communicate program specifications to computer programmers
- test and implement computer programs and provide user training
- plan and implement computer security systems for database access control
- analyze databases.

The main users of the services of computer consultants are computer consulting firms and computer systems units throughout the private and public sectors.

Educational Consultant

Consultants in this field:

- evaluate curriculum programs and recommend improvements
- develop the structure, content, and objectives of new programs
- conduct statistical analyses to determine the cost-effectiveness of education policies and programs
- provide ongoing professional development, training, and consultative services to teachers
- develop teaching materials and other resources for program delivery
- conduct research and produce reports pertaining to education policies and programs.

Educational consultants are engaged mainly by government departments, school boards, and education research institutes.

Energy Consultants

Energy consultants conduct research, prepare reports, provide consultation and advice, and assist in the administration of programs related to the energy field.

These consultants offer their services mainly to federal, provincial, and municipal governments, private companies, and advisory and consulting agencies.

Financial Consultants

Consultants in this category:

- collect financial and investment information about companies, stocks, bonds and other investments using daily stock and bond reports, economic forecasts, trading volumes, financial periodicals, securities manuals, company financial statements and other financial reports and publications

- examine and analyze financial and investment data collected, including profiles of companies, stock and bond prices, yields and future trends and other investment information

- provide investment advice and recommendations to clients

- prepare company, industry, and economic outlooks, analytical reports, briefing notes, and correspondence.

These consultants offer their services to a wide range of establishments throughout the private and public sectors, including banks, insurance companies, investment companies, manufacturing firms, utility companies and trust companies.

Human Resources Consultants

Human resources consultants:

- develop, implement, and evaluate personnel and labour relations policies, programs, and procedures

- advise managers and employees on the interpretation of personnel policies, benefit programs, and collective agreements
- research and prepare occupational classifications, job descriptions, and salary scales
- research employee benefit and health and safety practices and recommend changes or modifications to existing policies.

Consultants in human resources are engaged by a wide variety of organizations throughout the private and public sectors.

Interior Design Consultants

Interior design consultants:

- consult with clients to determine needs, preferences, and purpose of space
- develop detailed plans and models showing the arrangement of walls, dividers, displays, lighting, and other fixtures
- develop decorating plans and advise on selection of colour schemes, floor and wall coverings, furniture, and other items
- estimate costs and materials required
- prepare specifications for the final interior designs.

Architectural firms, interior design firms, retail establishments, construction companies, and other establishments are the main users of the services of interior design consultants.

Marketing Consultants

Marketing consultants:

- develop strategies and programs to promote industrial and commercial products

- conduct surveys and analyze data on the buying habits and preferences of wholesale or retail consumers

- conduct comparative research on marketing strategies for industrial and commercial products.

Marketing consultants are engaged mainly by government agencies, marketing firms, advertising agencies, and business associations.

Nutrition Consultants

Consultants in this category:

- provide nutrition counseling and consulting to health professionals, dietetic interns, community groups, government, media and individuals

- plan, evaluate and conduct nutrition education programs and develop educational materials for students and the general public

- participate on health care teams to determine nutritional needs of patients and to plan therapeutic diets and menus

- study and analyze current scientific nutritional studies and conduct research to improve the nutritional value, taste, appearance and preparation of food.

Nutrition consultants offer their services mainly to hospitals, nursing homes, government agencies, industry, and educational institutions.

Sports Consultants

Sports consultants:

- provide expert advice and consulting services to community groups, corporations, schools, and other organizations in the design and development of sports programs

- conduct research and develop policies related to sports.

The main users of the services of sports consultants include health and sports organizations, community centers, recreational institutions, and sports and fitness consulting firms.

Travel Consultants

Consultants in this field of consulting:

- provide travel information to clients regarding destinations, transportation and accommodation options, and travel costs

- plan and organize vacation travel for individuals or groups

- provide travel tips regarding tourist attractions, foreign currency, customs, languages, and travel safety.

Travel consultants offer their services mainly to travel agencies, transportation and tourist firms, and hotel chains.

WHY PEOPLE ENGAGE THE SERVICES OF INDEPENDENT CONSULTANTS

Independent consultants are used because they provide valuable services to governments, private organizations, and individuals. It may seem reasonable to you for an individual who is just establishing a small business to use the services of an independent business consultant to advise him or her on the different aspects of setting up a business. But why does a government or a huge multi-national organization, with so many experts in so many fields engage the services of independent consultants? Let's explore the reasons.

1. Independent consultants provide temporary expert assistance.

A company may need to reform its organizational structure or revamp its marketing strategy. The company's executives may be quite capable of performing the tasks, but may be giving their full attention to the day to day management of the organization. In such circumstances, it makes sense to call in independent management and marketing consultants.

2. Independent consultants provide expertise

An organization may call upon the expertise of an independent consultant to provide advice when such expertise is lacking in the organization. For example, it may not make good economic sense for an insurance company to employ a computer specialist who would be idle most of the time. Instead, the company may call in an independent computer consultant whenever it requires expert computer services. Also, an independent consultant may be called in to train a particular staff in the use of new techniques.

3. Independent consultants provide fresh insights and impartial viewpoints

Very often, when I am observing a game of chess, I see good moves that the players can make moves that I would not have seen had I been playing the game. This seems to be the case with other things as well. A company's executives may be too close to a problem to see the solution. They may be 'set in their ways' and may find it difficult to approach problems and situations from new perspectives. An independent consultant is not encumbered by such attachments and can often add fresh insights to a problem and propose feasible solutions.

Additionally, the personal involvement of executives in the affairs and internal politics of their organizations often makes it difficult or impossible for them to be impartial. It may be advisable in such circumstances to call in independent consultants who are capable of rendering impartial advice.

4. Independent consultants provide authority, legitimacy and credibility

Because independent consultants are experts in their fields, their reports and recommendations are often regarded as being authoritative and credible. A business executive may call in an independent consultant so that the consultant's report or recommendations can lend authoritative support, legitimacy and credibility to a course of action that the executive wishes to take.

5. Independent consultants can raise funds

It is a myth that financially successful companies don't need to raise capital. A highly successful company can want to raise funds for expansion. Of course, new companies need start-up capital, and even well-established companies might need a cash transfusion to restore it to economic health. In all such circumstances, an investment consultant or a fundraising consultant may be just what the doctor would order.

6. Independent consultants can save clients' time

In a fast-paced society, individuals, private organizations, and governments are often operating on tight schedules, trying to meet deadlines. This report has to be finished to meet the upcoming board meeting, that analysis must be ready for presentation to the loan committee, and that brief must be finished for the meeting scheduled for next Thursday. Often, the only way to meet such deadlines is to use the assistance of independent consultants.

7. Independent consultants as crisis managers

Nothing inspires a client to call in an independent consultant better than a crisis. When there is serious trouble, call in an independent consultant. There are different types of crises:

- the lump that may turn out to be cancerous

- the roof that keeps leaking even after it has been patched up several times by the roofers

- the threat of bankruptcy and foreclosure

- the job loss that was thought to be only temporary, but seems to persist

- the drastic loss of market share

- the pending lawsuit.

What may be considered a crisis by one client may be regarded as only an inconvenience by another client. But once the situation reaches crisis proportion (in the mind of the client), it often sends the client searching for an independent consultant, usually in a frenzy or bewilderment.

CHAPTER SUMMARY

1. Independent consulting is the process whereby independent and knowledgeable people provide expertise to others for a fee.

2. The steps in the consulting process are problem identification, data collection, developing alternatives, selecting the best alternative, making recommendations, and evaluating results.

3. There are consultants in virtually all aspects of private, social, business, and public life. People become consultants for a variety of reasons including the possession of marketable skills, the need to earn a living, the expectation of extra income, and the prestige associated with consulting.

4. It is not necessary for an independent consultant to have a graduate degree. However, he/she must have expertise acquired either through formal education or through experience.

5. Independent consultants are engaged because they are able to assist private individuals, business organizations and governments to achieve certain objectives.

SELF-TEST QUESTIONS

Indicate whether each of the following is true (T) or false (F).

1. _____ By its very nature, consulting is a single activity that results in satisfying the needs of clients.

2. _____ Any professional who offers a service for a fee is an independent consultant.

3. _____ The role of independent consultants is to find solutions and make recommendations to their clients. They should do only that and not implement any recommendations.

4. _____ Consultants do not need to identify problems. Their clients already know what the problems are. The role of consultants is to solve, not identify, problems.

5. _____ Every consulting problem has one and only one solution. The independent consultant must use his/her expertise to find that solution.

6. _____ Independent consultants are the employees of their clients. They should therefore act in their clients' best interests.

7. _____ It is possible to succeed as an independent consultant even if you do not have a university degree. But you must have specialized knowledge and/or skill in your field.

8. _____ One of the advantages of independent consulting is the freedom to decide what to do and when to do it. The success of an independent consultant does not depend on decisions made by his/her employer.

9. _____ It is the responsibility of independent consultants to involve their clients in the consulting process, so that the probability of implementation of their recommendations will be enhanced.

10. _____ Once the consultant has made his/her recommendations, the assignment is finished. His/her job comes to an end.

11. _____ To become an expert in any particular field requires both years of formal education and years of experience.

12. _____ Independent consultants are employed by their clients from whom they receive consulting assignments.

13. _____ Independent consulting is limited to those fields which are not regulated and in which licensing is not mandatory.

14. _____ Internal consultants who are employed within particular organizations to provide expert advice exclusively to the organizations that employ them are not considered to be independent consultants.

15. _____ Factors that motivate people to become independent consultants include the desire for independence, the need to earn a living, the expectation of extra income, and prestige.

16. _____ It is possible to be a successful independent consultant on the strength of love of independence, expertise, and a desire to succeed.

17. _____ An advanced degree from a recognized educational institution is a necessity for an independent consultant because such a degree provides credibility.

18. _____ Years of experience and special talent may contribute to an individual's expertise in a particular area, and cause him/her to become a successful independent consultant, even if he/she may not have a high level of formal education.

19. _____ In many cases, an independent consultant's place of work is determined by the field in which he/she consults.

20. _____ In order to become an independent consultant, one must have expertise in a wide range of areas. Expertise in a single field will not be enough.

21. _____ Governments and large multi-national corporations do not engage the services of independent consultants because they are able to employ experts.

22. _____ A cost-conscious company will not engage the services of consultants to perform tasks that its own staff can perform.

23. _____ The personal involvement of business executives in the affairs and internal politics of their organizations often makes it difficult or impossible for them to make objective decisions.

24. _____ A business executive may call in an independent consultant so that the consultant's report or recommendations can lend authoritative support, legitimacy, and credibility to a course of action that the executive wishes to pursue.

25. _____ A highly successful business organization that is making a great deal of money will have no need to raise funds.

26. _____ Independent consultants are hardly ever called upon during crisis situations because most people attempt to deal with crises in their own way.

ANSWERS

1. F   2. F   3. F   4. F   5. F   6. F   7. T   8. T

9. T   10. F   11. F   12. F   13. F   14. T   15. T   16. T

17. F   18. T   19. T   20. F   21. F   22. F   23. T   24. T

25. F   26. F

CHAPTER 2
THE CONSULTING BUSINESS

INTRODUCTION

This chapter continues our study of the consulting business. It examines several important issues other than those discussed in Chapter 1. The chapter begins with the organizational structure of an independent consulting business, and the importance of having an appropriate organizational structure.   If you are not particularly familiar with organizational design, perhaps you could engage the services of someone who is familiar with this area of work.   Your consulting business should be organized in such a way that it facilitates decision-making by the different decision-making units in your organization.

The chapter then turns to a discussion of security in the consulting business, examining the factors that affect the independent consultant's security.   New areas for independent consulting are considered, and some attention is given to monetary concerns.   We pay considerable attention to the important issue of ethics in the consulting business, the limitations of consultants, and the interaction between consultant and client. The chapter ends with a short list of consulting associations and resources on the Internet.

THE ORGANIZATIONAL STRUCTURE OF AN INDEPENDENT CONSULTING BUSINESS

A consulting firm, like other organizations, has objectives that it would like to accomplish. A suitable organizational structure will contribute to the efficiency of a consulting business. An independent consulting firm may consist of a single consultant doing all the work by himself/herself. At the other extreme is the huge national or international consulting firm hiring hundreds of consultants and supporting personnel. Whatever the situation may be, a solid organization is one of the keys to success.

For the purpose of this discussion, we shall consider a consulting firm that is organized as a single proprietorship. We assume that the single proprietor engages the services of other independent consultants when the need arises, and employs an Executive Assistant who also performs clerical duties. Figure 2.1 depicts the organizational structure of the hypothetical independent consulting firm. Other arrangements, of course, are possible. For example, the hypothetical consulting firm could employ consultants as employees of the firm. In this case, they would not be *independent* consultants as we have defined the term.

The single proprietor functions as Chief Executive Officer (CEO). He/she is totally responsible for the operation of the firm. Directly under the CEO is an Executive Assistant who reports to the CEO.

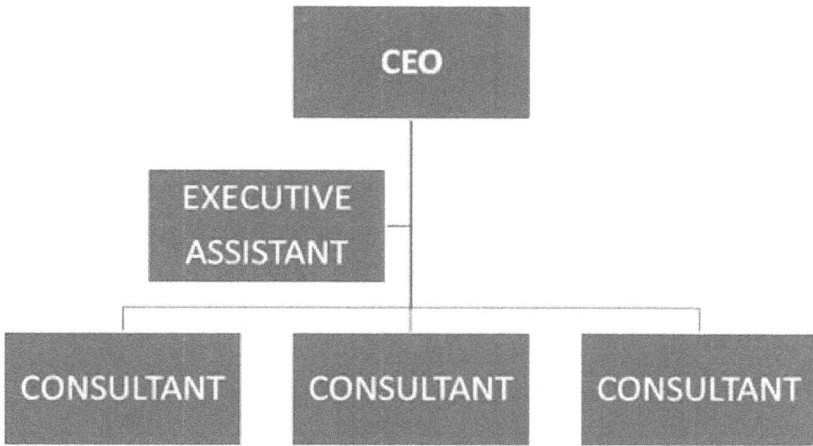

Figure 2.1. Organization Chart for a Hypothetical Consulting Firm

The chart shows three consultants who report directly to the CEO.

SECURITY IN CONSULTING

How secure is a career in independent consulting? There are not too many industries that can compare with the consulting industry in terms of security. We shall consider the following sources of security for independent consultants:

- changes in economic conditions
- changes in technology
- governments
- changes in lifestyles.

Changes in Economic Conditions

When the economy is experiencing a recovery or expansion, employment and income grow, prosperity is in the air, and individuals and organizations are in a position to afford to pay for the services of independent consultants. During recessionary periods, unemployment increases, people become increasingly uncertain about the future, and personal and business bankruptcies increase. Such economic downturns and waning fortunes cause people to depend on the services of consultants to get them out of trouble.

The foregoing is not to suggest that all types of consulting services are immune to economic fluctuations. On the contrary, the demand for particular consulting services will fluctuate with fluctuations in general economic activity. For example, when the economy is expanding rapidly and it is easy for workers to find employment, consultants who specialize in counseling the unemployed on how to find employment will experience a contraction in their business. On the other hand, the demand for consultants who specialize in finding workers for industry will increase, and the consultants in that field will experience an expansion in their businesses.

Changes in Technology

Changes occur in rapid succession in our modern world. You are probably familiar with the saying, "Change is the only constant." The fact that our society is constantly changing provides an element of security for the consulting industry. One of the implications of rapid technological change is that a large segment of society will lack knowledge about many things necessary for a comfortable existence, and therefore need to rely on the services of independent consultants.

A single example will suffice. Consider the various ways in which the Internet and the World Wide Web have affected our lives. Consultants in this field can help us to adapt to these drastic changes, so the demand for such independent consultants will increase.

But it is also true that rapid changes in technology can threaten the security of certain independent consultants. For example, independent consultants in accounting, who are incapable of making, or who simply fail to make, the transition from manual to computerized accounting will soon find their practices facing serious threats of extinction. This suggests that independent consultants need to be absolutely up to date with developments in their fields in order to avoid becoming obsolete.

Government

Governments are some of the biggest users of independent consulting services. The economic and social ramifications of new laws must be studied, the impact of new tax measures on government revenues and on the economy in general must be determined, and governments need a great deal of information about just about everything in order to formulate public policy. In short, the existence of governments adds security to the careers of independent consultants.

Changes in Lifestyles

The days when everyone was a "jack of all trades" are long gone. Our world has become much more interdependent. There have been significant changes in lifestyles and in the way we get things done. Today, there are many functions that we do not perform for ourselves either because we do not know how to do them or because we do not want to do them. Accordingly, we rely on specialists to assist with our weddings, to advise us about our investments, to advise us on tax matters, to advise us on our wardrobes, and to advise us about interior decorating. Our changing lifestyles strengthen the security of independent consulting.

NEW AREAS FOR INDEPENDENT CONSULTING

New opportunities for independent consultants are emerging. In this section, we look at a few of these new and emerging areas. With a bit of imagination, you will be able to come up with a few of your own.

In his book, "Boom, Bust and Echo," Canadian author David Foot alludes to certain changes in demography that can open up new opportunities for independent consultants. Although Foot's demographic study deals mainly with demographic changes in the Canadian population, his conclusions are relevant and applicable to many other places where similar conditions prevail.

Foot reminds us that as a given population ages, its focus changes to different types of activities. According to Foot, walking and gambling are going to get even bigger than they already are now, so here are opportunities for walking and gambling independent consultants.

Foot suggests that as people grow older, gardening becomes a popular activity. Gardening consultants should be prepared for the increased opportunities. And what about golf? Good opportunities for independent consultants in this field.

Foot cites bird watching as a candidate for the fastest-growing sport in the country (Canada), and predicts a growing television audience resulting from demographic changes. Are you contemplating a career as a television viewer consultant, advising viewers how to get maximum satisfaction from television viewing? Well, what about a career as a bird-watching consultant?

AND NOW, THE MONEY

Consulting is not a "get rich quick" scheme. Having established that fact, we can now turn our attention to the question of how much money an independent consultant can expect to make. One ought not to be so naive as to think that no one has ever entered the consulting business "just for the money." However, the vast majority of consultants will declare, truly, that money is not the primary reason behind their desire to become independent consultants.

In many ways, independent consultants are just like other people. They eat, some of them pay rent, some of them have mortgages to pay, they all wear clothes (most of the time), some of them own cars and have children to support and educate, and like other people, they enjoy going on vacation. All these things require money, and some of them require lots of money. So even if money may not be the overriding motive for entering the independent consulting field, it is certainly an important consideration.

The amount of money that you can make as an independent consultant depends on two key factors: price and volume. Let us first consider price. The price that you can charge for your consulting services is a function of many factors, including:

- the nature of your expertise (i.e., your field);
- the characteristics of your clients;
- the type of competition you face; and
- your reputation as a consultant.

All these factors will be discussed in detail in Chapter 4 dealing with the pricing of independent consulting services.

A brief discussion of the other key determinant of the independent consultant's income, viz., volume, is in order. Volume here refers to the amount of work you get. Like price, it also is a function of many factors. The independent consultant needs to recognize the crucial relationship between price and volume. You can literally price yourself out of the market (i.e., get no clients) by charging a price that is out of the reach of even the most wealthy clients. At the other extreme, you can charge a price that is so low that it will be impossible for you to handle the volume of work. Of course, this could mean a lot of work but little or no money. Moreover, a ridiculously low price might convey the message that your services are inferior, hence you may get very few clients.

Effective marketing is one means whereby independent consultants can exert some control over their volume of work. For example, appropriate advertising and other forms of promotion can often increase work volume. Chapter 3 discusses in some detail, how to market independent consulting services.

Some consulting firms regularly bill their clients for millions of dollars each year. Some independent consultants make a great deal of money annually while others merely get by. Depending on your area of expertise and your reputation, you might be able to charge an *hourly rate* (if you choose that option) of $75 or $300 or more. Chapter 4 discusses pricing methods in detail.

CONSULTING ETHICS

Ethics may be defined as systems of beliefs about what is right and wrong (morals) that are generally accepted by a group of people. Some actions that are accepted as right by one group may be condemned as wrong by another, and what may have been regarded as acceptable behavior at one time may be frowned upon at another time. Indeed, right is always in season, but what is right may be seasonal.

The success of independent consultants depends critically on their credibility. A credible independent consultant draws clients like a magnet; an independent consultant who has lost credibility will quickly cease to be a consultant. The independent consultant's credibility can be severely tarnished by unethical behavior.

Independent consultants face ethical issues in their work daily. The major problem in the area of consulting ethics is not so much the black-and-white issues but the grey areas. Most independent consultants would not face an ethical dilemma if asked to write up a false report that would result in the loss of human lives. They would refuse on ethical and moral grounds. That would be a black-and-white issue.

Now, consider the following case. A consultant has accepted an assignment from A & R Foods (a fictitious company) to study the company's operation and make recommendations to management about increasing A & R's market share. Shortly thereafter, Foods Unlimited (another fictitious company), a competitor, offers the same consultant a similar assignment. Should the consultant accept the second assignment? Different consultants will answer this question differently. This is an example of a grey area in consulting ethics, and it is issues like these that face the independent consultant on a regular basis.

Let us consider another example. Many organizations offer a simple assignment to a consultant, and based on the consultant's performance on that assignment, may offer larger and more complex assignments. Suppose an organization engages your services for a simple assignment. Your performance on that assignment is superb, and on that basis, the organization decides to engage you for a more complex assignment and is willing to pay you a substantial sum of money. However, the assignment is beyond your capabilities. Do you take the assignment and muddle through? Do you accept the assignment and farm the work out to another consultant, or do you decline the engagement?

This is another example of a grey area in consulting ethics.

Consulting practices will be ethical or unethical to the extent that consultants are ethical or unethical. In other words, if independent consultants are ethical, then their practices will be ethical. Unfortunately, a particular behavior may be considered ethical by one consultant and unethical by another. To deal with this particular problem, consulting associations have developed ethical codes of conduct for their members. These codes are designed to guide the behaviour of consultants, especially in those "grey areas" discussed earlier. Nevertheless, violations of these codes are not uncommon.

The ethical code of conduct endorsed by The International Institute for Independent Consultants (TIIIC) is listed below.

Confidentiality

Any information obtained about a client should be kept confidential. Not only should you not pass the information on to anyone else, but you should not use it for your personal profit, unless you obtain permission from the client.

Interest Priority

The clients' interest must take priority over the interests of the consultant. Although you are not your clients' employee, you are expected always to act in your clients' best interest.

Conflict of Interest

Independent consultants should not accept assignments that place them in a conflict of interest situation. For example, the Institute considers it unethical for a consultant to accept assignments from competing clients if his/her recommendations to one client place the other at a disadvantage.

Honesty

Independent consultants should deal honestly with their clients at all times. Honest dealing increases the consultant's credibility.

Fee Disclosure

Independent consultants should disclose to their clients, in advance, all fees associated with assignments, and the manner in which payment should be made. Consultants should never *surprise* clients with their bills.

Competence

Independent consultants should accept only those assignments that fall within their scope of competence. They should offer services with competence and integrity.

Objectivity

Independent consultants should approach their assignments with as much objectivity as possible. Consultants should inform their clients of any threats to their objectivity as soon as they are detected, and offer to withdraw from an assignment if they are incapable of offering objective advice.

Misleading Advertising

Independent consultants should not knowingly engage in misleading advertising. In some jurisdictions, even today, lawyers are not allowed to advertise, other than by a sign discretely displayed at the outside of their offices, for fear of ethically questionable advertising. The code of conduct of the European Federation of Associations of Management Consultants regards advertising in a blatant or commercial manner as being "unprofessional conduct."

Efficiency

Independent consultants should try to solve their clients' problems as efficiently as possible. They should not prolong an assignment in order to benefit financially from such willful delays.

Professionalism

Independent consultants should always conduct themselves as professionals. They should avoid commenting on the work of their colleagues, especially if the comments are negative.

NOT EVERYTHING CAN BE FIXED

It is often said (and there is more than a grain of truth in it) that every problem has a solution. In fact, that tenet is accepted at my consulting firm. However, that's not the same thing as saying that everything can be fixed. Some things cannot be fixed. A leaking roof is a problem with a solution. It may not be possible to stop the leak by fixing the roof. Instead, the solution might be a new roof. As another example, a business might be in so much trouble that the only practical solution is to have the business declare bankruptcy. Consultants cannot fix everything because they are not God.

However, before you decide whether or not a problem can be fixed, you must first diagnose the problem. Many examples can be cited where consultants claimed that certain situations could not be remedied, when in fact, there were often rather straightforward solutions. A successful consultant is one who has the ability to search for solutions by examining alternatives, and who is smart enough not to accept to fix something that cannot be fixed.

If you cannot solve the client's problem after carefully studying the situation, then you should let the client know. One of my clients offered me an assignment to increase his sales revenue by 15% in one year. Given the budget he was prepared to allocate to the project, and the quality and quantity of his sales staff (among other things), his objective of a 15% increase in sales revenue was highly unrealistic. Needless to say, I declined the offer.

The point that I am trying to make here is that if you know that you cannot meet your client's objectives, if you perceive that the problem cannot be fixed, if you are asked to perform the impossible, don't touch the assignment. Decline gracefully and professionally.

CONSULTANT CLIENT INTERACTION

In accepting an assignment from a client, the independent consultant enters into an important relationship with the client who might be an individual, a group of individuals, or representatives of an organization. For the purpose of this discussion, we will assume that the client is an organization rather than an individual. The independent consultant interacts with people within the organization at various levels.

Often, the consultant is brought in by top management personnel or by the board of directors. There is an individual (usually an executive officer) with whom the consultant discusses the assignment and who receives the consultant's report. If the assignment is to be successful, the consultant must develop a good working relationship with this individual.

Depending on the nature of the assignment, it may be necessary for the consultant to interact with the board of directors. Although they may not be directly involved in the day-to-day management of the organization, the board is ultimately responsible for setting its overall direction and for ensuring that established goals are accomplished.

Independent consultants want to see their recommendations implemented. There is no guarantee that a report will not end up on a shelf in an office and be forgotten. But even in cases where serious attempts are made by management to implement the consultant's recommendations, the ultimate success of the engagement may be put in jeopardy.

More often than not, the success of an engagement (including successful implementation and the ultimate solution of the problem) requires the involvement and commitment of all employees of the organization.

The successful independent consultant must be able to enlist the full support of the employees. If the employees (especially those who must work closely with the consultant) perceive the presence of the consultant as a threat, they could very well sabotage the project. The consultant must therefore gain the confidence of the employees and relate to them in a non-threatening way. He/she must also understand group dynamics.

If feasible, at the beginning of an assignment, the consultant should arrange to meet with the employees of the organization. If the number of employees is too large to make this meeting practical, then information explaining the presence of the consultant should be circulated in writing to the people in the organization. Management should make a formal introduction of the consultant to the people with whom the consultant will interact most during the assignment. Once that is done, it is up to the consultant to use his/her human relations skills to develop a harmonious relationship.

During the course of the assignment, depending on the nature of work to be done, the consultant may have to make frequent intrusions upon the employees' time. The consultant may need to collect various types of data relevant to the assignment, and may have to conduct interviews with management personnel and employees. All this must be done discretely and with minimal disruption of operations.

Business executives may be reluctant to release certain types of information to the consultant. There is no need for the consultant to request such information unless it is required to solve the problem. If the information is really required, the consultant should tactfully and convincingly inform the executive that the information is crucial to the solution of the problem, and that by withholding the information, he/she may be doing serious damage to the organization. This will usually be enough to elicit cooperation.

The presence of an independent consultant working in an organization for an extended period of time is bound to generate curiosity and perhaps anxiety among some management personnel. Since the consultant is there to help to improve performance, some executives might interpret his/her presence as an attempt to highlight their inefficiency. In order to dispel these curious and anxious feelings, the consultant can suggest the timely and selective dissemination of information about the work being done to the affected group. Interim reports perform this function reasonably well.

A harmonious consultant-client relationship is beneficial to all concerned. The managers obtain the assistance they need without the added stress of conflict and friction with the consultant. Other employees are able to perform their normal functions without experiencing undue anxiety, and the consultant has a good chance of having his/her recommendations successfully implemented, with the prospect of additional engagements from the organization.

CONSULTING ASSOCIATIONS AND RESOURCES ON THE INTERNET

The independent consulting industry is becoming increasingly organized. This is evidenced by the number of independent consulting associations that have emerged over the years. Most of these associations provide one service or another to independent consultants. The following is a partial list of websites that you might find useful.

Institution	Website
Canadian Association of Management Consultants	https://www.cmc-canada.ca/
Institute of Management Consultants	https://imcusa.org/
The Management Consultancies Association (MCA)	www.mca.org.uk
The Society of Professional Consultants	www.spconsultants.org
International Council of Management Consulting Institutes (ICMCI)	www.cmc-global.org
The Consultancy Network	https://theconsultancynetwork.co/

Resources for Consultants on the Internet

Independent consultants will find useful resources for their practice at the following sites.

About Work	www.aboutwork.com
Companies Online	www.companiesonline.com
Consultant's Corner	www.pwgroup.com/corner
Expert Marketplace	www.expertmarket.com
Fast Company	www.fastcompany.com
Inc. Online	www.inc.com
Independent Consultant Resources	www.look4it.se
InfoWizard	www.infowizard.com

The foregoing is just a sample of useful information on the web. Consultants are in the information business, and one valuable source of information is the Internet and the Wide World Web. You should make use of them.

CHAPTER SUMMARY

1. A suitable organizational structure will contribute to the efficiency of a consulting business. An organization chart illustrates the structure of the organization.

2. Despite certain threats, the consulting business enjoys relative security from changes in economic

conditions, changes in technology, the existence of governments, and changes in lifestyles.

3. Demographic changes may bring about new opportunities for independent consultants.

4. An independent consultant's income depends on the price he/she is able to charge and the amount of work that he/she can get.

5. Consultants must be wary of ethically questionable situations and try to avoid them. Most consulting associations have developed ethical codes of conduct for their members.

6. A harmonious relationship between the independent consultant and his/her client is crucial for the success of most consulting assignments.

7. The Internet and the wide world web are good sources of information for independent consultants.

SELF-TEST QUESTIONS

Indicate whether each of the following is true or false.

1. _____ It is a myth that only large consulting firms with many consultants handling a wide variety of tasks need a solid organizational structure.

2. _____ During good economic times, the services of independent consultants are required. During bad economic times, the services of independent consultants are also required.

3. _____ Although changes in technology can increase the security of independent consultants, it is also true that rapid technological changes can threaten the security of certain independent consultants.

4. _____ The consulting business has developed to the stage where there are absolutely no areas left for new consulting services.

5. _____ According to Canadian author David Foot, independent consulting in an area such as gambling will never happen because of ethical issues.

6. _____ Most independent consultants will readily admit that money was the primary motive behind their decision to enter the consulting field.

7. _____ Your reputation as a consultant has a great deal of influence on the price you can charge and the number of clients you get. These are the key determinants of your income from consulting.

8. _____ Provided that an independent consultant can attract a large clientele, he/she is guaranteed a great deal of money.

9. _____ Lowering price is an effective way to get more clients, but it may not generate additional income.

10. _____ The fee that a consultant can charge for his/her services is a function of (that is, depends on) his/her reputation.

11. _____ A practice that was considered unethical at one time may be considered ethical at some other time.

12. _____ Ethical codes of conduct are designed to guide the behaviour of consultants. Violations of these codes are very rare.

13. _____ The International Institute for Independent Consultants considers it unethical for a consultant to accept assignments from competing clients if his/her recommendations to one client places the other at a disadvantage.

14. _____ It is not the responsibility of independent consultants to offer objective advice. Their duty is to offer advice which, in their opinion, is good for their clients.

15. _____ It is the responsibility of independent consultants to expose inefficiency and inadequacy in the work of other independent consultants.

16. _____ Independent consultants are interested not only in finding solutions to their clients' problems but also in seeing their recommendations implemented.

17. _____ Most often, it is necessary for consultants to interact only with top management personnel. The involvement of other employees is most often not required.

18. _____ The ultimate success of a consulting project may be hampered even if serious attempts are made by management to implement the consultant's recommendations.

19. _____ One way for consultants to obtain required information from an executive is to inform the executive that by withholding the information, he/she may be doing serious damage to his/her own organization.

20. _____ Consultants should always try to obtain as much information as possible, even if the information may not be required to solve the problem. It is always better to collect the information even if it may not be used.

21. _____ If a consultant has to work at the business place of a client, an explanation of the consultant's presence should be given to the employees.

22. _____ Interim reports often help to dispel the anxious feelings of workers who may view the presence of consultants as showing up their inefficiencies.

23. _____ Although there are so many independent consultants, very little or no attempt has been made to organize them.

24. _____ Independent consultants should avoid using any information from the Internet because such information is unreliable.

ANSWERS

1. T   2. T   3. T   4. F   5. F   6. F   7. T   8. F

9. T   10. T   11. T   12. F   13. T   14. F   15. F   16. T

17. F   18. T   19. T   20. F   21. T   22. T   23. F   24. F

CHAPTER 3
MARKETING CONSULTING SERVICES

INTRODUCTION

No matter how knowledgeable and experienced you may be as an independent consultant, your practice will not be successful unless you can effectively market your consulting services. Unless people are using your services, you are not consulting.

This chapter focuses on marketing your consulting services, that is, getting your services to the intended users, viz. your clients. In other words, the main thrust of this chapter is how to get clients. We will begin our discussion with a definition of marketing. We will then touch briefly on the marketing concept and marketing functions. Finally, we will spend a considerable amount of time discussing the sales letter as a means of reaching potential clients.

DEFINITION OF MARKETING

The American Marketing Association defines marketing as *"the performance of business activities that direct the flow of goods and services from producer to consumer or user."* Marketing then would include such activities as:

- advertising
- merchandising
- promotion
- pricing
- selling
- transportation

We define each of the following concepts as follows:

Advertising is any paid form of nonpersonal presentation, or promotion of ideas or products.

Merchandising is the process of selecting, displaying, and promoting products in a distribution outlet.

Promotion refers to various short-term selling efforts including contests, discount coupons, introductory offers, and special displays designed to increase sales of a product.

Pricing refers to the various strategies used to establish the price of a product in order to make it more appealing to customers.

Selling is the art or technique of personal persuasion employed to convince others to purchase a product.

Transportation is the term used for the physical transfer of products from sellers to buyers.

Clearly, all these different marketing activities will not carry the same weight when dealing with independent consulting services. For example, although the independent consultant can engage in merchandising to a limited extent, selling and advertising would be of much greater significance.

THE MARKETING CONCEPT

Over the years, the concept of marketing has shifted from a product orientation to a sales orientation to a new concept involving a customer orientation, a profit orientation, and an integration of marketing activities.

Customer Orientation

Customer orientation means determining what customers want and then allowing the wants to guide the suppliers' activities. From the perspective of the independent consultant, it means listening to the client and then offering solutions to the client's problems.

Profit Orientation

Economists have, for a long time, assumed that the primary objective of most business enterprises is to maximize profits. But profits are generated because firms cater to the needs and wants of society. Thus, if the independent consultant can convince clients that his/her consulting services will increase productivity, efficiency, and profitability, save time, or bestow some other benefits to the clients, they are more likely to engage the services of the consultant.

Integration

The new marketing concept emphasizes the coordination of all business activities new product development, advertising, sales, and financial activities. Even before production begins, the final user, the consumer, is brought into the picture. Information about customers' needs is collected and used to direct production decisions.

MARKETING FUNCTIONS

Marketing activities (selling, advertising, transportation, etc.) are contained in six broad marketing functions. Some degree of familiarity with these marketing functions will be useful in your endeavor to market your consulting services. The marketing functions are listed below:

> Market analysis
> Marketing communication
> Market segmentation
> Product differentiation
> Valuation
> Exchange

We shall briefly discuss each of these functions.

Market Analysis

The participants in a market are the buyers and sellers. Sellers offer goods and services for sale to customers. Your clients want you to know what their needs and wants are so that those needs and wants can be satisfied. You, as a seller of consulting services want to know what your clients and potential clients want. Market analysis allows you to know who your potential clients are and where they can be found.

Marketing Communication

Information is necessary for good decision-making. Marketing communication is the flow of information between buyers and sellers. Buyers are able to communicate their needs and wants to producers (sellers) who then offer the products to satisfy the expressed needs and wants. You communicate with your potential clients through such means as personal selling, advertising, and publicity.

Market Segmentation

You cannot sell your consulting services to all people. If you are a computer consultant, you will be wasting your time trying to sell your service to someone who does not have and does not intend to own a computer. Your potential clients will be people who are connected to computers in some way. You need to identify the segment of the market on which you will concentrate. That is the meaning of market segmentation. Your marketing activities will be targeted to a particular group.

Product Differentiation

Product differentiation is the term used to refer to the various methods employed by producers to make their products appear to be different from those of their competitors. If you were the only financial consultant in a certain market area, there would be no sense in trying to differentiate your service. But there is relatively strong competition in the consulting business. It is to your advantage to be able to convince potential clients that your services are different from your competitors' in ways that will more appropriately cater to their particular wants. The whole purpose is to develop a preference for your services.

For a tangible product, product differentiation can be achieved through distinctive design, packaging, labeling, or appearance. For consulting services, it can be achieved mainly through quality and pricing. For example, you could try to differentiate your services by stressing excellence, and the ability to meet deadlines.

Valuation

Before a client decides to engage the services of an independent consultant, he/she compares the benefits with the costs. Valuation is this process of cost-benefit analysis. The consultant also engages in valuation. He or she decides whether the benefits from offering the services are worth the costs. If the consultant can convince the client that the benefits outweigh the costs, the client is likely to use the services.

Exchange

The ultimate objective of marketing is to get the client to use the services of the consultant   to exchange services for money. The consultant delivers the service, perhaps in the form of a report, and the client pays for the service.

THE MARKETING MIX

The controllable variables that you will combine (mix) to satisfy your clients form the *marketing mix*. The marketing mix is usually discussed in terms of the four Ps:

> Product
> Place
> Promotion
> Price

Product Your product must be directly related to your target market. If your consulting service does not satisfy the needs of your clients and potential clients, you cannot have a successful consulting practice.

Place Where and when will your clients use your services? This is an important question from the point of view of marketing. Your services must be available at a time and place where your clients can use them. In other words, you must consider the distribution channels to be used in getting your consulting services to your clients. Clearly, this is a more crucial problem in marketing goods than in marketing services, but it cannot be neglected.

Promotion You must make certain arrangements to communicate with your target market. Your prospective clients must have some way of knowing about your services. Methods of communicating with potential clients will be discussed below.

Price Consultants charge a fee for their services. In other words, a price is attached to the consultant's work. The price must be such that your clients will accept it. It must also be such that you receive adequate compensation for your expertise.

It is important to recognize that the four Ps are equally important in the marketing mix. Promotion is not more important than the product because without the product, there is nothing to promote. Neither is the product more important than promotion because unless you promote your product, it will not reach your clients. A similar equality can be worked out for all the Ps in the marketing mix.

WHAT IS YOUR PRODUCT?

When you enter a hardware store, you know what you expect to find there. Similarly, when you enter a grocery store, you know what you expect to find there. These stores are stocked with scores of merchandise from various producers. They are selling a wide variety of tangible products. You can evaluate these tangible products by their appearance, by their shapes, by the way they are packaged, and by other visible features. The same is not true of services.

SERVICES ARE UNIQUE

As an independent consultant, you are not selling a tangible product; you are selling a service. It is true that your advice may be presented in the form of a written report, but you are selling a service, not a tangible product. The fact that you are not selling a tangible product means that many marketing techniques that are effective in marketing goods (tangible products) may be ineffective in marketing services.

Services encompass four unique elements referred to as the **four I**s of services. These are:

1. intangibility
2. inseparability

3. inventory peculiarity
4. inconsistency

Let us examine each of these elements briefly.

Intangibility

The element of intangibility that sets services apart from goods (tangible items) presents a challenge for the marketing of services. Since you cannot physically add color to, change the taste of, or modify the shape of your consulting services, the alternative is to show clients and potential clients the benefits to be derived from using your services. One garage proclaims its service as "Service you can trust."

Inseparability

In many cases, the consumer separates the good from the manufacturer of that good. He or she may not even know who produces the item. In the case of independent consulting services, the client identifies the services with the consultant. In the client's mind, the provider of the service and the service itself are inseparable. This suggests that your *personal* qualities will feature significantly in a client's decision to use your consulting services.

Inventory Peculiarity

Some goods are perishable and others have high storage and handling costs. If a fall in demand results in an undesirable increase in inventory, the producer responds by reducing production and perhaps selling off some of the inventory at reduced prices (an inventory sale). As an independent consultant, inventory accumulation manifests itself in idle time. The implication for marketing is obvious. Your inventory cost is very high.

Inconsistency

Automation and computerization are two factors that have contributed to the consistency of goods. Whether the quality of goods is excellent, average, or inferior, mass production methods tend to make tangible products consistent. Of course, there may be one or two defective items in a production batch, but by and large, there will be consistency or standardization.

In the case of independent consulting, the same degree of consistency is unlikely. The independent consultant's training and experience will tend to reduce inconsistency, but they will not eliminate it. Today, you are as sharp as a whip, and you solve your clients' problems with relative ease. Tomorrow, your performance is not bad, but it is not up to your usual standard. This inconsistency in service makes clients somewhat uncertain as to the quality of service they will receive, and tends to make them reluctant to use the service. Service inconsistency presents a challenge for the marketing of consulting services.

Evaluative Qualities

In marketing your consulting services, it is useful to know how consumers evaluate their purchases. Tangible products can be evaluated on the basis of color, style, size, shape, etc. The consumer can search until he/she finds the items with the desired shape, color, or size. These qualities of tangible products are referred to as *search* qualities and can be determined before purchasing the item.

Certain goods and services such as restaurant meals and haircuts have *experience* qualities that can be determined only during or after the use of the service. Independent consulting services do not possess search qualities. To a certain extent, they possess experience qualities. Mostly, however, they possess what is referred to as *credence* qualities which are difficult to evaluate. It is often difficult or impossible for a client to determine whether or not, and to what extent, a consultant is offering sound advice. This creates uncertainty in the client's mind and makes it difficult to sell consulting services.

What is Your Product?

Earlier in this chapter we asked the question, What is Your Product?" It is an important question. The independent consultant must have a clear picture of what service he/she is offering, otherwise the marketing process will be blurred, a target market will be difficult to identify, and the consulting practice may suffer.

Your Mission Statement

One means of zeroing in on your product is through a *mission statement.* A mission statement defines your business *exactly* and *precisely.* It is a clear statement of the purpose of the business   the reason for its existence. A mission statement will help you answer the questions, "What is my product?" and "Who are my potential clients?"

A major designer and manufacturer of electronic products and systems for measurement and computation has the following mission:

To provide the capabilities and services needed to help customers worldwide improve their personal and business effectiveness.

A public utility company states:

Our mission is to work for the success of the people we serve by providing our CUSTOMERS reliable electric service, energy information, and energy options that best satisfy their needs.

Finally, consider the mission of The International Institute for Independent Consultants:

To provide certification for independent consultants in any field in any part of the world through distance learning.

Let us analyze the mission statement of The International Institute for Independent Consultants.

1. The raison d'être of the organization is clear: "To provide certification..."

2. The market that the organization wishes to serve is clearly defined: "independent consultants in any field."

3. The geographical area or extent of the market is specified: "in any part of the world."

4. The method to be used is stipulated: "through distance learning."

Independent consultants who are interested in certification, or who can be persuaded about the importance of certification would be potential clients. The service is not confined to the local market, but through distance learning, to the global market.

MARKETING METHODS

A variety of marketing methods that can be successfully used to market consulting services are listed below. They include:

> Sales letters
> Brochures
> Business cards
> Selected media advertising
> Conducting seminars
> Writing a book
> Using the Internet

We shall discuss the sales letter below, and in the next chapter, we will discuss the other marketing methods.

THE SALES LETTER

Of all the methods of reaching potential clients, direct mailing (sales letters, brochures and business cards) are the most selective. Once you have identified your target group (market niche) you can shoot directly at that segment of the market. This is the greatest advantage of the sales letter as a marketing tool. The selectivity of sales letters allows you to reach the age group, the professional group, the geographical area, etc. that are potential users of your consulting services.

As a direct result of the selectivity of your mailing list, the sales letter is the least expensive method per potential client. With this method, you do not spend money to reach people who are not likely to be interested in your services. This is an advantage as well as an important consideration from the viewpoint of budgetary control.

Another advantage that can be claimed for the sales letter is that it has the capacity to capture the full attention of the reader. Once the letter has grabbed the reader's attention, there is no competition from other items for his/her attention. With a newspaper advertisement, for example, there are other items and pictures on the page, vying for the reader's attention. Such is not the case with a sales letter.

If you are not particularly good at writing effective sales letters, you should consider using the services of an experienced copywriter. The service will cost you a few dollars, but it will be money well spent.

The Effectiveness of the Sales Letter

Sales letters tend to be most effective when used to sell products of a specialized nature and products that are fairly expensive. Since consulting services are specialized and fairly expensive, they seem to lend themselves to selling by the sales letter.

Desirable Features of the Sales Letter

In order for the sales letter to be effective in obtaining favourable action from the reader, it must be structured in such a way as to:

1. Attract the reader's attention

2. Arouse interest

3. Create a desire for the service

4. Facilitate action.

We refer to these features of the sales letter as the AIDA prescription where **A** represents *attention,* **I** represents *interest,* **D** represents *desire,,* and the final **A** represents *action.*

1. Attracting Attention

Whether your sales letter will be read or tossed into the waste paper basket depends on the first few sentences of the opening paragraph. If the opening paragraph grabs the reader's attention, you have a chance of getting your message across to the reader. Since the opening sentence of the sales letter is so crucial, let us spend some time examining *attention getters.*

Relevant Question   A relevant question is an effective way of attracting attention and arousing curiosity:

> *How much money did you save last year?*

> *How long does it take you to read a two-hundred-page book?*

Since everyone is interested in saving money, the reader who is asked the first question is likely to read on. Busy people who can't afford to spend a great deal of time reading a book would be curious about what is to follow from the second question.

Courteous Command   If used properly, a courteous command can be an attention-getter:

Wait a minute! Don't through this into the waste basket yet.

If you are completely satisfied with your accountant, don't waste your time reading this letter.

Human Interest Story   Would an opening statement like the one below motivate you to read on?

I was deeply touched last week by the story of the eight-year-old girl who saved her pet's life.

Important Facts   A statement of a significant fact can be used to attract attention.

Last year, ABC Consulting reported an increase of 30% in its client base.

Surprise   Surprises can be effective as openers, but they have to be used judiciously.   Would the following statement attract your attention?

Customers don't want good service; they want excellent service.

You should try to compose some attention grabbers and ask yourself how you would react to them.

2. Arousing Interest

Once you have attracted the reader's attention, your next task is to turn that attention to your advantage. Your letter must arouse the reader's interest. This can be done in several ways, but a very effective way is to appeal to the reader's emotions. For example, if you are a financial consultant writing to a prospective client about financial planning, you can appeal to his/her emotions by referring to the importance of providing for one family in the future. For example, the following statement will arouse interest:

> *You would not like to know that in years to come, your loved ones will face tremendous financial hardships ....*

3. Creating Desire

What causes people to desire a service? There are numerous reasons, but we shall consider only a few. You can safely assume that potential clients will be inclined to use your service if it helps them to:

- make or save money
- save time
- avoid difficulties
- get out of trouble
- improve their appearance
- attract the opposite sex
- improve their performance
- improve their health
- protect themselves and their families
- sleep peacefully at nights

This section of the sales letter focuses on the client.

> *We know that you want to base your business decisions on pertinent facts.*

> *A diagnostic analysis will pinpoint both the strengths and weaknesses of your system and offer practical and affordable solutions.*

In this phase of the sales letter, you need to convince your reader that any claims made in your letter are true and supported. Facts and expert testimony are the main devices used for this purpose.

> *Since we started our consulting practice over 15 years ago, we have served a long line of satisfied clients who use our services repeatedly. Some of our recent clients include The XYZ Corporation, The O.K. Auto Mart, The Better Buy Furniture Store, Excompro, ...*

Note how effective the testimony of a distinguished person can be:

> *"Dr. John Andrews, Managing Director of Excompro, and Professor of Finance at East West University, says: 'We have used several consulting firms but we have been impressed mostly by the excellent quality of service given by ConsultSol. We will certainly continue to use their services.'"*

The testimonies of past users can also be convincing:

> *I have learned more in this two-day seminar about --------- than I have learned in an entire semester at university.*

4. Facilitate Action

The sales letter should end with a suggestion for the reader to act. The easier it is for the reader to act, the greater the probability of success of the sales letter will be. For example, a stamped and addressed envelope or a no-charge telephone call is appropriate. Consider the following closing paragraphs:

Your signature on the enclosed card is all we need to send you the information, free of charge.

Order your copy NOW by signing and returning the enclosed card.

The Use of PostScript

How often do you pay attention to the P.S. at the end of a letter? If you are like most people, the answer is, "Nearly always." P.S. then can be used effectively to prompt action.

If you call our toll-free number 1 800 123 4567, or write to us, we will mail you a free copy while quantities last.

An Example of a Sales Letter

The following sales letter demonstrates the use of devices to attract attention, create desire, convince the reader, and facilitate action.

Dear Mr. Edwards:

On September 5, 19 , I received a memorable call from one of my clients the Manager of a small manufacturing company with 27 employees. He had called to express his gratitude to me and my staff for our diagnostic analysis and recommendations that have transformed his firm from a company that was struggling to pay its bills into a healthy profit maker.

It is not our practice to submit unsolicited proposals to potential clients, but we know that many small and medium size firms are unduly limiting their profit potential, and we know that we can help.

Our comprehensive diagnostic analyses have:

- *increased sales by 53% in one insurance company after only four months*
- *reduced costs by over 6% in one manufacturing company*
- *increased sales for a manufacturing firm from $19 million to $24.7 million in less than one year, while raising net profits by more than 15%.*
- *increased average labor productivity by more than 5.5 % in one printing company.*

I hope that you will take a few minutes to study the enclosed proposal and that you will take full advantage of our service to strengthen the financial position and profitability of your company.

Sincerely yours,

John Thomas
Managing Partner

P.S. We have recently prepared a special booklet, Pricing for Profit, for our clients. If you call or write, we will be pleased to send you a complimentary copy, while they last.

The *attention grabber* used here is curiosity. How many small business managers would not be curious to know the reason for the call? Not many. Note how the second sentence leads to creating a desire for profit, which is further intensified in the second paragraph. The exact statistics of benefits from a diagnostic analysis derived by specifically identified businesses are designed to convince the reader. Note the effective use of a P.S. as an incentive for action. The statement "while they last" creates a sense of urgency.

CHAPTER SUMMARY

1. Marketing is the entire process by which goods and services flow from producers (providers) to users (clients). It involves activities such as advertising, promotion, pricing, transportation, etc.

2. The new marketing concept focuses on meeting clients' needs, making a satisfactory level of profit, and the coordination of business activities.

3. Marketing functions include market analysis, marketing communication, market segmentation, product differentiation, valuation and exchange.

4. The marketing mix centers around the four Ps of marketing: product, place, promotion and price.

5. Before you can effectively market your consulting services or services, you must first have a clear picture of precisely what it is that you are offering.

6. A mission statement can help you specify exactly what service or services you are offering.

7. Several marketing methods are available to independent consultants. These include, among others, sales letters, brochures, selected media advertising and seminars.

8. In marketing your consulting services through the use of sales letters, you should try to attract the

reader's attention, arouse interest, create a desire, and facilitate action. This is the AIDA recipe.

SELF-TEST QUESTIONS

Indicate whether each of the following is true or false.

1. _____ Marketing activities will be superfluous if you provide excellent service because your service will market itself.

2. _____ Marketing activities include advertising and promotion as well as pricing and transportation.

3. _____ One difference between advertising and selling is that advertising is non-personal while selling is personal.

4. _____ The new marketing concept has a customer orientation and a profit orientation coupled with a focus on the integration of marketing activities.

5. _____ To be a successful independent consultant, you must try to sell your consulting services to all people.

6. _____ Product differentiation refers to the practice of selling many different products to many different categories of customers.

7. _____ One can achieve product differentiation in consulting services through quality and pricing.

8. _____ With reference to the marketing mix, the four Ps include patience, practice, profits, and people.

9. _____ In the marketing mix, the four Ps are equally important.

10. _____ Marketing techniques that are effective in marketing goods will also be effective in marketing services.

11. _____ Services possess four unique elements: intangibility, inseparability, inventory peculiarity, and inconsistency.

12. _____ One of the great advantages of being an independent consultant is that clients quite easily separate the consultant's personal qualities from the services that he/she is offering.

13. _____ Because consulting services are intangible, they are easier to market than tangible products.

14. _____ Search qualities are properties such as style, size, colour, shape, etc. for which clients can search until they find items that fit the bill.

15. _____ Independent consulting services possess experience qualities to a certain extent, but they mostly possess credence qualities that are difficult to evaluate.

16. _____ A mission statement expresses the reason for the existence of an organization. However, it is totally unrelated to marketing, especially marketing consulting services.

17. _____ Direct mailing is the most selective of all methods of reaching potential clients.

18. _____ The main disadvantage of the sales letter as a marketing device is that it is the most expensive method per potential client.

19. _____ An advantage that can be claimed for the sales letter is that it has the capacity to capture the full attention of the reader.

20. _____ Since consulting services are specialized and fairly expensive, they seem to lend themselves to selling by the sales letter.

21. _____ In marketing, the acronym AIDA means attitude, important, direct, and awareness.

22. _____ In setting his/her consulting fee, a consultant must consider whether the fee will provide adequate compensation for his/her expertise. Whether or not the fee (price) will be accepted by the client is not an important consideration.

23. _____ The consultant must have a clear picture of what he/she is offering in terms of services, otherwise it will be difficult to identify a target market.

24. _____ A question such as "How much profit did you make last year?" as the opening of a sales letter to a business person is likely to be a real "turn off" because most business people would regard such a question as an intrusion.

25. _____ Courteous commands, important facts, relevant questions, and human interest stories are all effective ways of attracting a reader's attention.

26. _____ Once you have attracted the reader's attention in a sales letter, and aroused his/her interest, there is really no need to try to convince him/her of any claims made in the letter.

27. _____ One of the most effective ways of arousing interest in people is to appeal to their emotions.

28. _____ Using testimonies of past clients to promote one's consulting practice is unethical and should not be done. It is a violation of confidentiality.

29. _____ A postscript should never be used in a sales letter because it detracts from the main purpose of the letter which is to get the prospective client to become a client.

30. _____ It is a good idea to end a sales letter with a suggestion for the reader to act, and to make it easy for him/her to comply.

31. _____ Readers are often convinced by the use of relevant statistics, provided that they are not overwhelmed by such statistics.

ANSWERS

1. F   2. T   3. T   4. T   5. F   6. F   7. T   8. F

9. T   10. F   11. T   12. F   13. F   14. T   15. T   16. F

17. T   18. F   19. T   20. T   21. F   22. F   23. T   24. F

25. T   26. F   27. T   28. F   29. F   30. T   31. T

CHAPTER 4
OTHER MARKETING METHODS

INTRODUCTION

In the previous chapter, we discussed certain basic principles of marketing as a means of providing a framework for studying the marketing of consulting services. In that chapter, we listed several marketing methods and discussed the sales letter in some detail.

In this chapter, we turn our attention to other marketing methods that independent consultants can use. In particular, we discuss the capability brochure, business cards, the Yellow Pages, selected media advertising, seminars, publishing a book, using the internet, and other marketing devices.

THE CAPABILITY BROCHURE

A capability brochure can be an effective means of reaching prospective clients. New consultants, however, tend to exaggerate the importance of brochures in their consulting practice. Any experienced consultant will tell you that, contrary to opinions held by new consultants, a brochure is NOT the central point in marketing your service. My viewpoint is supported by Thomas Greenbaum, who, in his book, *The Consultant's Manual,* has pointed out that many successful consultants do not have a brochure.

It may not be necessary to begin your practice with a brochure, but you may eventually feel the need for a brochure. While such a brochure is an effective marketing tool, its effectiveness depends on how it is used. In this author's opinion, the brochure is most effective when it is used *after* (not before) an initial contact has been made with the prospective client. If a client makes inquiries about your services, then it is most appropriate to provide him/her with a copy of your brochure.

Having established the proper use of the brochure, let us proceed to an examination of its appearance, size, and contents.

Appearance A dingy, shabby-looking brochure probably does more harm than good to a consulting business. The brochure should be attractive and well laid out. It should reflect who and what you are by its very appearance. No matter how valuable the information it contains may be to prospective clients, it will not get through to them unless the brochure has some compelling appearance that provides an incentive for the recipients to read it.

Is color necessary? There is no doubt that color enhances the appearance of the brochure. However, color printing is very expensive, so the consultant has to weigh the added benefit of color against the cost. Another factor to consider is that an expensive-looking brochure printed in color on glossy paper suggests that your services are high priced. Although this may not necessarily be the case, that is the message that is usually conveyed. There is no guarantee that a high-priced, glossy, multicolor brochure will be more successful than a simple brochure that is quite presentable.

Size Brochures come in all sizes   from the massive 25-page or more to the single folded sheet. The size of your brochure depends on the objectives you want to accomplish and on the particular characteristics of the market being targeted. Most independent consultants want a brochure that is relatively simple and can be included with a direct sales letter.

Content Remember that you are using your brochure to advertise your consulting business and to convince prospective clients that they cannot do better than engaging *your* services. For this reason, your brochure should specify your services precisely and explain what it is that sets you apart from your competitors.

As a minimum, your brochure should contain the following information:

Nature of Business
List of Services
Examples of Past Work
Examples of Benefits Derived from Your Services
Qualifications and Experience
Any Special Relevant Accomplishments

List of Recent Clients
Where and How to Reach You

Our purpose in this chapter is not to give instructions on the development and production of brochures. Instead, we are more interested in presenting the brochure as a marketing tool. From that perspective, let us review the sections of the brochure listed above.

Nature of Business

The brochure should begin with a precise descriptive overview of your consulting practice, stating when and specifically why it was established. It is a good idea to include your mission statement as this device clearly and succinctly states the purpose of your business.

List of Services

Many independent consultants offer more than one service. For example, a management consultant may offer services in accounting, marketing, business organization, etc. Even in cases where the practice appears to be a one-service business, it can be presented as offering more than one service. For example, a tax consultant may consider that he or she offers only one service: a tax service. In fact, the brochure could list services such as completion of income tax forms, pick up and delivery, same day service, tax planning, etc.

Examples of Past Work

From a marketing standpoint, citing examples of past work in the brochure is significant. Prospective clients would want to know what specific work you have done in the past. Would you rush to be the first patient of a brain surgeon? If a client is engaging you to advise him or her on preparations for a wedding, that client would have a lot more confidence in you if he/she knows that you have done that kind of thing before.

Examples of Benefits

This is an opportunity for you to use your brochure to convince the prospective client to use your services. If you can make a legitimate and honest claim of some benefit that the user will derive, it becomes much easier to sell your service.

Qualifications and Experience

Remember that as an independent consultant, you are an expert in your field. You have acquired specialized knowledge and skills through education, training, and experience. Use this as a selling point. In addition to your own qualifications and experience, you can capitalize on the qualifications and experience of other key people in your organization (if appropriate). This is one means of building the credibility of your consulting practice.

Special Accomplishments

If you or others in your organization have won national or other awards or have made great accomplishments in your area of consulting, it is advantageous to mention them in this section of your brochure. It reflects upon who you are and will help to market your services.

List of Clients

It is acceptable to list current and recent clients that you are serving or have served. If there are some well-known clients on the list, it will help your cause. It is also helpful to state briefly what you have done for each client. For example, International Trustco (prepared procedure manuals); and Sun Valley Community Hospital (successfully performed executive search).

Where to Reach You

The ultimate objective of the brochure is to get clients. You have given the readers (prospective clients) some information about your company and the services that you offer. Hopefully, you have convinced them that it is worth their while to use your services. Now, you must let them know how and where they can reach you. This section usually closes the brochure. The office location, a phone number, a fax number, or an e-mail address should be included here. If you have a web page, it can be listed.

Example of a Capability Brochure

In order to give you an idea of how the items discussed above may be included in your brochure, we provide an illustration of a capability brochure for a hypothetical consulting firm. In the same way that each consulting firm is unique, so too is each capability brochure. Although you may get ideas by examining capability brochures of other firms, you cannot copy the details of those brochures and expect to come up with a brochure that is specific to your firm.

Illustration 4.1. Capability Brochure

NEW AGE CONSULTING

COMPANY BACKGROUND

New Age Consulting *is an international consulting firm providing a wide variety of consulting services to senior management personnel both nationally and internationally. Established in 1968, the firm has extensive experience and has developed considerable expertise in assisting business enterprises of all size, as well as to not-for-profit organizations.*

In over 30 years of continuous and successful engagements, our practice has grown from a modest staff of three to its present complement of more than twenty highly qualified consultants. New Age has established a fine reputation for excellent performance on major assignments, and for providing individual attention to the needs of clients.

New Age has a track record of success that has earned the patronage of many long-term clients and the respect of our professional colleagues. We can conduct a detailed analysis of your company's operation and offer solutions to your business problems.

OUR MISSION

New Age *is fully committed to providing its clients with the best possible counsel. The complete satisfaction of our clients is guaranteed by our full commitment to excellence in service.*

We will make a difference

OUR ORGANIZATION

For organizational efficiency, the firm is divided into six units, each headed by a Director who reports directly to the Vice President. Directors are responsible for consultants who supervise their assistants. The firm is headed by the President who is the Chief Executive Officer. The Project Coordinator overseas all projects and reports directly to the President.

Note: A copy of your firm's organization chart may be included here.

The following table shows the six units and the specific areas of consultation for which each is responsible.

Units and Their Responsibilities

Unit	*Responsibilities*
Accounting/Finance	*Accounting and finance problems, domestic and offshore company registration.*
Economics/Business	*Feasibility studies, business plan development, business and economic forecasting, economic and market research, and publications.*
Human Resources	*Human resource development, human resource management, job analysis and job evaluation, human relations problems.*

Marketing/Public Relations	*Marketing problems, market analysis and research, public relations, and image building.*
Management/ Organization	*Strategic management, motivation, organizational structure and design, organizational development, company manual production.*
Technical Services	*Computer programming, web page design, and maintenance.*

LIST OF SERVICES

New Age Consulting is adequately prepared to offer a wide variety of specialized services to its business and non-business clients.   In providing these services, our primary goal is the satisfaction of our clients. Among the services that we offer are the following:

- *Accounting*
- *Business plan development*
- *Feasibility studies*
- *Financing*
- *Forecasting*
- *Human resources development*
- *Human resources management*
- *Job evaluation & salary administration*
- *Marketing*
- *Organizational structure and design*
- *Production of company manuals*
- *Public relations*

- *Research*
- *Web page design*

A brief description of our services follows:

(You describe your services now).

OUR PERSONNEL

To ensure that our clients obtain only top-quality services, we employ top-ranking consultants who are highly skilled and experienced in various aspects of business. With degrees from fully accredited colleges and universities, and professional experienced acquired from major corporations, our consultants are eminently qualified to deliver prompt, efficient, and effective solutions to your problems.

OUR APPROACH

Although the specific approach followed will depend on the nature of the assignment, New Age has nevertheless established broad general principles for carrying out our assignments.

Once an assignment has been accepted, we do the following:

- *Assemble a team for the project*
- *Collect <u>pertinent</u> preliminary information, using our short Company Data Questionnaire*
- *Prepare and present to the client, a proposed Work Schedule and Work Flow Diagram*

- *Conduct a comprehensive and constructive examination of the organizational structure, department, or organization, its plans and policies, its financial controls, its methods of operation, and its use of human and non-human resources. The main objective of this audit is to reveal strengths as well as weaknesses, and to indicate and to indicate possible improvements.*

- *Involve management and staff in the process to the fullest extent possible to ensure the success of the project.*

- *Use a team approach on all assignments to arrive at the best possible solution.*

OUR CLIENTS

New Age offers its services to small, medium-sized, and large business enterprises and organizations. It is a compliment to New Age that most of our engagements have come through referrals from satisfied clients. Our clients include:

Add a list of recent clients (for example, banks, insurance companies, airline companies, etc).

EXAMPLES OF PAST ASSIGNMENTS

Within the past few months, we raised $500,000.00 for one client, installed a job evaluation system for another client, performed organizational diagnostic analyses for several clients, redesigned the organizational structure for *two companies, and developed business plans for several companies.*

OUR CODE OF PROFESSIONAL CONDUCT

(List your code of professional conduct here, if you have one).

HOW TO REACH US

For more information, please feel free to contact us. New Age will be glad to accommodate you at your convenience.

> *New Age Consulting*
> *P.O. Box 123*
> *City, Prov./State*
> *Country*
> *Tel: (000) 123-4567*
> *Fax: (000) 123-6789*
> *e-mail: nac@newage.com*

We invite you to visit our website at: www.newage.com

BUSINESS CARDS

Business cards are a *convenient* means of promoting your consulting business. It is much more professional to be able to reach into a neat business card holder for a business card to give to a client or prospective client, or even a suspect than to write the information on a piece of paper. Don't leave your home or your office without a few of your business cards.

You should not hand out your business cards indiscriminately at inappropriate times and places. Not only is such an action unprofessional, but it may also be considered to be in poor taste. When someone asks for your card, or during an introduction, it is quite appropriate to offer your business card. Whenever you offer your card, do so discretely.

It is also a good idea to enclose your business card with communication sent from your office. While a letter may be filed remotely or may be read and then discarded, there is a good chance that your card will be placed in a business card file for later reference. Your business cards should have a professional appearance. Remember that these cards represent who you are. Therefore, they should be of high quality. If your budget allows it, go for the raised print on your business cards. The statement that your cards make is important, and you do want them to speak of high class and professionalism.

Never lose sight of the fact that your business cards are a part of the marketing process. As such, they must convey pertinent information. Your card should carry the following information:

Name of company
Your name, including designation (if applicable)
Your position in the organization
A logo (if you use one)
A descriptive term that defines your service
Business address
Business telephone and fax numbers
e mail address

The information on the card should be arranged in such a way as to make reading easy. Consider the following two examples of business cards illustrated in Figure 4.1.

Card #1

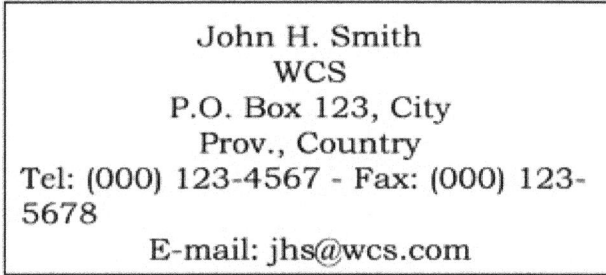

John H. Smith
WCS
P.O. Box 123, City
Prov., Country
Tel: (000) 123-4567 - Fax: (000) 123-5678
E-mail: jhs@wcs.com

Card #2

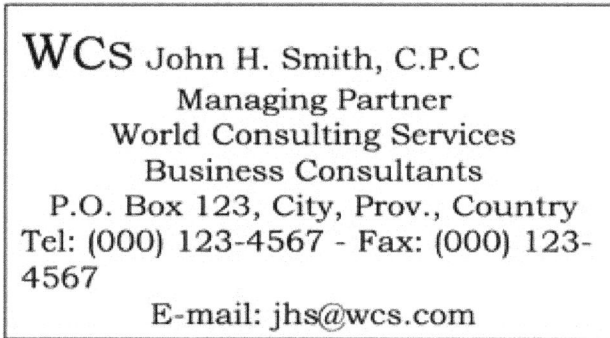

WCS John H. Smith, C.P.C
Managing Partner
World Consulting Services
Business Consultants
P.O. Box 123, City, Prov., Country
Tel: (000) 123-4567 - Fax: (000) 123-4567
E-mail: jhs@wcs.com

Figure 4.1. Examples of Business Cards

Card #2 displays some important features that are not contained in Card #1.

1. Unless WCS is well known, it has no meaning to the reader. Card #2 spells out the meaning.

2. Card #2 offers a brief description of the service, "Business Consulting."

3. The C.P.C. designation presumably refers to some kind of certification. It adds credibility.

4. The position of the individual (Managing Partner) is indicated.

Keep these features in mind when you design your business cards.

THE YELLOW PAGES

The usefulness of *The Yellow Pages* in today's digital age has diminished significantly, though it retains niche value in certain circumstances. Many *Yellow Pages* publishers have shifted their focus to online directories, offering searchable databases and digital advertising opportunities. Examples include **Yellow Pages Digital** in the U.S. and **Yell.com** in the UK. However, printed versions are increasingly becoming obsolete as the world moves further into a digital-first approach.

I have often been asked by independent consultants whether or not it is advisable to take out an advertisement in the Yellow Pages of the telephone directory. My response has always been that it depends on the type of consulting business in which one is engaged. If you are offering your services to a more general clientele, an advertisement in the Yellow Pages may be a good idea. If you are serving a more specialized clientele, then the advantage of such an advertisement is questionable.

If you do decide to advertise in the Yellow Pages, bear in mind that larger advertisements are more effective than smaller ones. This conclusion is based on the psychological fact that people tend to associate large advertisements with large companies and small advertisements with small companies. My personal advice on this matter has always been: "Try a large advertisement in the Yellow Pages for one year. If it does not generate calls, discontinue the advertisement and simply maintain the usual Yellow Page listing.

SELECTED MEDIA ADVERTISING

Note: Some professional and consulting associations prohibit certain types of advertising by their members. Be aware of what is acceptable practice in your profession or association.

Advertising in the media newspapers, magazines, trade journals, radio, and television can be effective if properly selected. The emphasis is on proper selection.

Newspapers

Except for a few special types of consulting services (e.g., executive search consultants), newspaper advertising is hardly ever successful. This fact may be surprising to those who confuse the "total reach" of the medium with potential clients. It must be remembered that the objective of the advertisement is not to reach as many *people* as possible but to reach as many *potential clients* as possible. A newspaper may have a large total reach, being read by a large number of people. But perhaps not many of those readers are potential clients.

Magazines and Trade Journals

These media tend to be more specialized than newspapers and may therefore be more effective vehicles for reaching clients. In choosing the magazines or trade journals in which you will place your advertisement, the prime consideration should be your target market. It would make sense for a gardening consultant to place an advertisement in a magazine that is devoted to gardening. Similarly, it makes sense for a management consultant to advertise in a management journal.

Radio and Television

Radio and television are terrific media for reaching large numbers of people. However, if these media are used, you need to be selective in terms of the programs on which you choose to place your advertisements. A fair amount of the programming on talk radio and TV is designed to attract particular types of audiences and viewers. For example, a fitness consultant could benefit considerably by advertising on a fitness show, and an educational consultant could advertise successfully on an educational talk show.

The Advertising Copy/Script

Like the sales letter, the advertisement is designed to get a specific response from potential clients. Like the sales letter, it should attract attention, arouse interest, create a desire, and prompt action (remember the AIDA formula). Because the typical advertisement is much shorter than a sales letter, it is more difficult to accomplish these objectives in the typical advertisement. If you decide to use media advertising, and if you are not a good copywriter, you should consider using the services of an experienced professional copywriter.

CONDUCTING SEMINARS

Seminars can be so successful in getting clients that many consultants give free seminars. Let us assume that a financial consultant decides to give a one-day seminar on "Principles of Investing." The attendees at this seminar will, most likely, be people who are interested in investing, either because they have funds to invest, or because they want information that will be useful to them in the future when they have funds to invest. Clearly, this is a fertile spot for potential clients.

If you decide to give such a seminar, be sure to hand out material with your business name, address, and telephone number. Invariably, some attendees will approach you on some issues that they would like to pursue further. Seize the opportunity to give them your business card with a suggestion to call you at the office.

PUBLISHING A BOOK

The success of any individual consulting practice depends to a large degree on the extent to which the consultant is considered an expert. The more you can convince clients and potential clients of your expertise, the greater the probability that they will use your services. Publishing a book on a particular subject tends to identify you as an authority on the subject and adds several notches to your credibility. Many of my clients have sought my services solely based on the fact that I have published several books in the area of my consulting.

USING THE INTERNET

More and more people are turning to the Internet as a source of information. Depending on your area of consulting, you might find this medium an appropriate vehicle to reach clients. If your prospects are likely to have access to the Internet, then you may consider designing a web page or having one designed for you. Remember that the objective is to get clients, so your web page should use the AIDA formula discussed earlier. Don't forget to include your e-mail address.

You will, of course, register your site with several search engines. In addition to having a web page, you can also advertise your consulting service on many places on the Internet. If you are not familiar with using the Internet as a marketing tool, you should seek the help of someone who does. It may be well worth your while.

OTHER MARKETING DEVICES

The foregoing does not exhaust the possible avenues available to you for reaching potential clients. The following are additional methods that might work for you.

Cold Calls

Cold calls are calls made on prospective clients with whom you have had no previous contact. It involves physically visiting potential clients either where they work or where they live, depending on the nature of your practice. If you are calling on business prospects, remember that you may have a tough time getting to see the person who has the authority to authorize work. So unless you are creative, you may not even get past the receptionist. Once you have managed to see the prospective client, make sure that (1) you know exactly what you want to say, (2) you leave your card and a brochure if you have one.

Being A Guest on Radio and TV

Guesting on radio and television gives you exposure and opens up opportunities for consulting assignments. You should never appear on radio and TV unless you are properly prepared. If you appear to be uncertain about your field, you will not inspire confidence. On the other hand, if you demonstrate knowledge and confidence, you could give your practice a significant boost.

Being Active in the Community

Taking an active role in worthwhile community affairs is one good means of building a good public image. Such an image is essential for success as an independent consultant. Many independent consultants have attracted clients by maintaining a high profile in their communities.

CHAPTER SUMMARY

1. A capability brochure, if properly designed and used, can be an effective marketing device. It seems to be more effective when used after an initial contact with a prospective client.

2. The brochure should contain information on the nature of the consulting business, services offered, past assignments, benefits derived from your services, qualifications and experience of your staff,

special relevant accomplishments, list of recent clients, and how to reach you.

3. High quality business cards are important. They should be well laid out with pertinent information.

4. Yellow Page advertisements may be effective if you are catering to a more general clientele. They seem to be less effective in reaching a more specialized clientele. Large advertisements tend to be more effective than small ones.

5. Newspapers, magazines and trade journals, radio and television can be effective, but proper selection is the key to their effectiveness.

6. Other means of reaching and obtaining clients include seminars, publishing a book, using the Internet, cold calls, guesting on radio and television, and maintaining a high profile in the community.

SELF-TEST QUESTIONS

Indicate whether each of the following is true or false.

1. _____ A capability brochure is not essential to having a successful consulting practice. A brochure could do more harm than good to a consulting practice.

2. _____ The effectiveness of a brochure depends more on how it is used than on whether or not one exists.

3. _____ What is important is what the brochure contains, not its outward appearance.

Clients couldn't care less about the appearance of the brochure.

4. _____ A brochure should be used to *inform* prospective clients of your services, not to *advertise* those services.

5. _____ It is unethical for independent consultants to include examples of past work and lists of recent clients in their capability brochures.

6. _____ It is a good idea to include your mission statement in your brochure because it clearly states the purpose of your business.

7. _____ One means of building the credibility of your consulting practice is to capitalize on the qualifications and experience of key people in your organization.

8. _____ It is advantageous to mention in your brochure any national or other awards that you may have won.

9. _____ National and other awards that you have won should not be mentioned in your capability brochure, since they are not likely to be of any interest to prospective clients.

10. _____ A popular company advertised its product using the slogan "Don't leave home without it." The same advice could easily apply to business cards.

11. _____ It may be unprofessional to hand out your business cards at certain times or at certain places.

12. _____ You should never enclose a business card with communication sent from your office.

13. _____ A business card is a useful device for introducing you and your business to prospective clients. It should not be viewed as a part of the marketing process.

14. _____ If a consultant is serving a highly specialized clientele, the advantage of advertising in the Yellow Page is questionable.

15. _____ Because newspapers have a large total reach, advertising consulting services in them is generally successful.

16. _____ Magazines and Trade Journals tend to be more specialized than newspapers and may therefore be more effective than newspapers in reaching clients.

17. _____ Cold calls are calls made on prospective clients very early in the morning before the day gets hot.

18. _____ It is always a bad idea for independent consultants to appear as guests on radio or TV, because such appearances give the impression that the consultants are desperate for clients.

19. _____ Publishing a book on a particular subject tends to identify you as an expert on the subject, but it does not enhance your credibility.

20. _____ Independent consultants are paid for their services, therefore, they should not give free seminars.

21. _____ The Internet is a great source of information for independent consultants, but it is also a good medium for reaching clients.

22. _____ Maintaining a high profile in the community is one means of building a good public image and enhancing your chances of success as an independent consultant.

ANSWERS

1. T   2. T   3. F   4. F   5. F   6. T   7. T   8. T

9. F   10. T   11. T   12. F   13. F   14. T   15. F   16. T

17. F   18. F   19. F   20. F   21. T   22. T

CHAPTER 5
THE MARKETING PLAN

INTRODUCTION

In the previous two chapters, we were concerned with marketing concepts and ideas as they pertain to consulting services, and with methods and devices that can be used to market consulting services.

The main purpose of this chapter is to emphasize the importance of a marketing plan and to provide you with some instructions as to how you can prepare a marketing plan for your consulting firm. We begin the chapter with a discussion of external and internal environmental factors that affect market planning. Then we define a marketing plan and point out some of the factors that are necessary for market planning. Next, we consider the minimum desirable features of a marketing plan. Finally, we take you step by step through the preparation of a marketing plan.

Before an individual actually establishes a consulting practice, he or she usually thinks seriously about the decision. Where is the start-up money coming from? Am

I going to get clients? What accounting books do I need? Should I hire a secretary? These are important decisions. Sometimes, the would-be consultant is wise enough to develop a business plan with a section containing a marketing plan. Regrettably, however, this planning process is often no more than a one-time exercise. Market planning should be an annual activity for the independent consultant.

ENVIRONMENTAL CONSIDERATIONS

Environmental factors will play an important role in developing a marketing plan for your consulting firm. Marketing and other decisions are not made in a vacuum. We must consider the environment in which such decisions are made. We must also consider how changes in the environment affect our marketing strategies. Some of the environmental factors are external while others are internal. In general, you will have little or no control over the external factors and will therefore have to accept them as given. On the other hand, you will be able to exert some measure of control over the internal factors.

The External Environment

The following external environmental factors should be considered in preparing your marketing plan.

Economic factors: You should monitor changes in economic variables such as gross domestic product (GDP) — the market value of all goods and services produced in the economy, the unemployment rate, trends in interest rates, bankruptcy statistics, etc.

Technological factors: Changes in technology have profound effects on economic activity, and we are living in an age of rapid technological changes. These changes affect the market for consulting services so you should consider them in your marketing decisions.

Legislation and Regulations: There are rules and regulations governing business activity. You should be aware of these laws that affect your consulting business. Changes in legislation may present an opportunity for you to market your consulting services.

Cultural and demographic factors: Population dynamics such as population shifts and changes in the age composition of the population may have significant implications for marketing your services. Cultural changes may also affect the demand for your services and affect your market planning.

Competitive factors: It is unlikely that you will be the only consultant in your area. You must therefore be aware of competition from other consultants. Furthermore, you must be aware of possible threats from potential new entrants into the consulting business and prepare a marketing plan that will outline strategies for dealing with such competitive threats.

The Internal Environment

The following are a few of the important internal environmental factors that should be considered in preparing your marketing plan.

Objectives: Your marketing plan is to help you to achieve specific objectives. The preparation of a marketing plan therefore presupposes the establishment of clearly defined objectives. Circumstances may dictate that you change your objectives, but this will not be problematic since you do have control over the objectives.

Human Resources: You must keep in mind that it is people who will implement your marketing plan. If you are the only person in your consulting firm, then you do not have the problem of coordinating human resources to implement your marketing plan. If, however, you employ other people in your consulting firm, they need to be aware of the plan and their expected role in its implementation.

Financial resources: In preparing your marketing plan, you must be aware of the financial needs of the consulting enterprise. The various marketing activities that will be outlined in your marketing plan will have to be financed. You will not have unlimited financial resources, but once the size of your budget has been determined, you do have some control over how much of it will be allocated to the various functions.

THE NATURE AND IMPORTANCE OF A MARKETING PLAN

Many independent consultants underestimate the importance and significance of a marketing plan in their consulting practice. Ironically, those same consultants often attempt to convince business clients of the importance of having a marketing plan.

One *now* prominent independent business consultant related to me how embarrassed he was when trying to convince a prospective client to use his consulting services to develop a marketing plan. His strategy was to create a desire by highlighting the tremendous benefits to be derived from a marketing plan. The consultant was making a great deal of progress with the sale until the prospective client asked: "Do you have a marketing plan for your consulting business?" The consultant did not have a marketing plan for his consulting business.

If you were planning to drive to an unfamiliar destination, one of the first things you would try to obtain is a *current* road map. Such a map could save you a great deal of time that might otherwise be lost in stopping for directions, making wrong turns, taking wrong exits, etc. A marketing plan is similar, in many ways, to a road map. It helps you to determine where you are now, where you want to go (i.e., what objective you want to achieve), and how to get to your final destination (i.e., what means you will use to accomplish the desired objectives). Therefore, a marketing plan is not just a fancy document designed only to impress financiers, shareholders and suppliers. It is a useful document designed to provide directions for the user on the road to building a successful consulting practice.

MINIMUM DESIRABLE FEATURES OF A MARKETING PLAN

The contents of marketing plans differ depending on the nature of the business and the entire marketing environment. As a minimum, however, a marketing plan should exhibit the following features:

1. Simplicity

A marketing plan should be simple and short. Although simplicity and brevity are desirable features, the marketing plan should not omit significant details pertaining to how particular objectives are to be accomplished.

2. Goal Oriented

A marketing plan should be goal oriented. Not only should goals be stated explicitly, but the plan should outline strategies to help you accomplish your mission.

3. Continuity

A marketing plan should provide for continuity. It should not be regarded as an end document. Instead, it should be a part of a process that permits future plans to build on it. In other words, each plan should be seen as a precursor of the next annual marketing plan.

4. Validity

Since the marketing plan will be used to guide your business decisions in the area of marketing your firm and your services, the assumptions upon which it is based should be valid. If you build a marketing campaign on the premise that the economy is expanding, then the economy should, in fact, be expanding. Ideally, the plan should be based on solid facts rather than on opinion. If solid facts are unavailable, then you should use your best judgement in estimating the information.

5. Flexibility

The conditions under which you operate your consulting practice are constantly changing. The marketing plan should be flexible in order to take account of changes in both the external and internal environment within which you operate. The assumptions upon which the marketing plan is based, though valid at the time of planning, may no longer be valid during implementation of the plan. Provisions must be made in the plan for such eventualities.

6. Realism

The marketing plan should be realistic in the sense that the various targets established should be attainable. It should be realistic also in the sense that it should be consistent with the resources available to you.

PREPARING YOUR MARKETING PLAN

Before you actually begin to prepare your marketing plan, there are certain facts that you will need. I have found that writing these facts on paper actually help. By answering certain key questions, you will collect the facts that are needed for the preparation of your marketing plan.

Table 5.1.   The Individual Consultant's Personal Market Planning Questionnaire

1. Who are (or will be) the users of my consulting services?

2. How much consulting services do they now use and who supplies their needs?

3. How many firms are offering the services that I offer (of plan to offer)?

4. Where are these firms located?

5. Can I identify any advantages or disadvantages that these firms have?

6. What prices do they charge?

7. What marketing methods and devices do they use to reach their clients?

8. Which methods seem to be most effective?

9. How has the market reacted to new entrants?

10. Can I distinguish between the most successful and least successful consulting firms?.

11. What factors account for this difference?

12. What do I want to achieve within the next six months, within the next year, within the next five years?

13. What special advantages do I have?

14. What disadvantages do I have?

15. How can I overcome these disadvantages?

It is possible that some of these questions may not apply in your particular case, and in other cases, it may be necessary to ask additional questions. The answers may not be so easy to come by, but the results will be well worth the effort. It is important to note also that the answers to these questions will not provide all the information needed to prepare a good marketing plan. But here is a good place to start.

Given the strategic importance of the marketing plan, you should give careful consideration to its preparation. The following steps illustrated in Figure 5.1 below are designed to guide you through the process.

Step 1. Situational Analysis

This step in the market planning process requires a description of the circumstances surrounding your decision to offer consulting services. Perhaps, for example, you saw an opportunity to satisfy a particular need. This section of the marketing plan should also describe present market conditions, including any possible marketing opportunities that may present themselves in the future. The situational analysis should contain information on the size of the market, its growth rate, its demographic features, pertinent government regulations, and competitive factors.

```
┌─────────────────────────────┐
│        SITUATION            │
│        ANALYSIS             │
└─────────────────────────────┘
              ↓
┌─────────────────────────────┐
│     TARGET MARKET           │
│     IDENTIFICATION          │
└─────────────────────────────┘
              ↓
┌─────────────────────────────┐
│       IDENTIFYING           │
│       STRENGTHS             │
│     & WEAKNESSES            │
└─────────────────────────────┘
              ↓
┌─────────────────────────────┐
│       GOAL SETTING          │
└─────────────────────────────┘
              ↓
┌─────────────────────────────┐
│         ACTION              │
│         PLAN                │
└─────────────────────────────┘
              ↓
┌─────────────────────────────┐
│     ASSIGNMENT OF           │
│     RESPONSIBILITY          │
└─────────────────────────────┘
              ↓
┌─────────────────────────────┐
│        BUDGETING            │
└─────────────────────────────┘
              ↓
┌─────────────────────────────┐
│       PROGRESS              │
│       EVALUATION            │
└─────────────────────────────┘
```

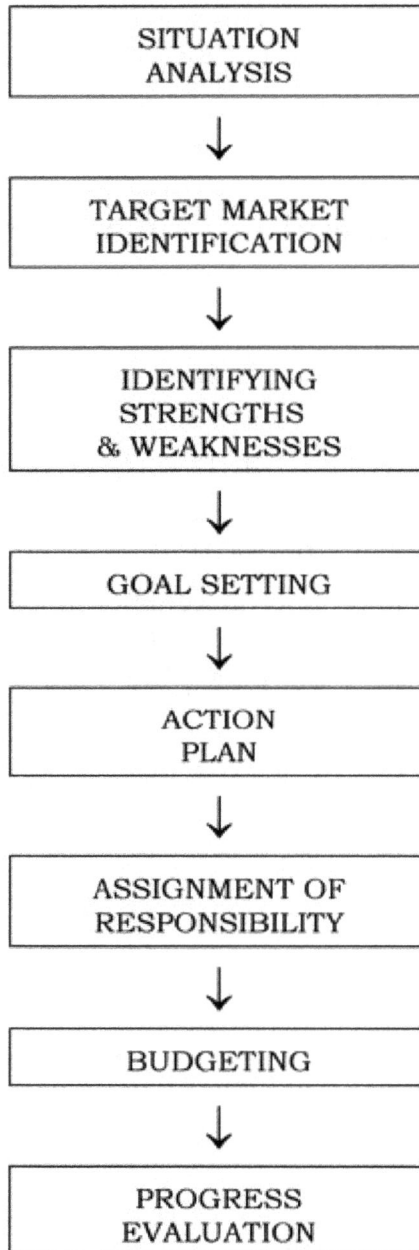

Figure 5.1. The Market Planning Process

Step 2. Target Market Identification

In this section of the marketing plan, you specify the segment(s) of the market that you propose to serve. In part, your area of expertise will help to determine your market segment. For example, if your expertise is in the area of adult education, your target market would naturally be related to the field of adult education.

Step 3. Identifying Strengths and Weaknesses

Having identified your market segment, you must then identify strengths and weaknesses in your service. A strength of your consulting service could be the ability to solve problems quickly. A weakness could be lack of time and resources to take on more than just a few assignments during a given period of time.

Step 4. Goal Setting

The next step in the process is the establishment of goals. These goals should be expressed in concrete terms. For example, instead of stating a goal as an increase in profits, it is preferable to state it in more concrete terms such as increasing profits by 10% over the previous year. Your goals could include increasing your client base by 20% by the end of the next year, increasing your total revenues from consulting by 15%, or adding a new service by a specific date. Remember that your goals and objectives must be realistic.

Step 5. Action Plan

In this section of your marketing plan, you outline the strategy that you will use to achieve your marketing objectives. For example, a strategy could be an increase in your advertising budget by 15% in order to increase your client base by 10%.

Step 6. Assignment of Responsibility

Here, you specify who will be responsible for the implementation of the marketing plan. The relevance of this step depends on the size of your consulting firm. If you are the only one in your firm, then the responsibility will fall squarely on your shoulders. If there are others in the firm, then the task should be assigned to someone who has the ability to perform the task.

Step 7. Budgeting

In this section of the marketing plan, you explain the allocation of funds to the various marketing activities. If financial resources are inadequate to allow for the implementation of the marketing strategy, then the plan may have to be modified or additional resources will have to be found.

Step 8. Progress Evaluation

The marketing plan is designed to help you to accomplish certain objectives in a specified period of time. You must evaluate the progress of your marketing efforts in order to determine the success of the plan. This type of monitoring allows you to make any adjustments that may be necessary.

CHAPTER SUMMARY

1. The market planning process requires a consideration of both external and internal environmental factors.

2. External environmental factors include economic factors, technological factors, legislative factors, cultural and demographic factors, and competitive factors.

3. Internal environmental factors include established objectives, your firm's human resources, and your financial resources.

4. A marketing plan is like a road map pointing out where you are, where you want to go, and how to reach your destination.

5. A marketing plan should be simple, goal oriented, have continuity, be valid, flexible, and realistic.

6. The steps involved in preparing a marketing plan are: situational analysis, target market identification, identification of strengths and weaknesses, goal setting, action planning, assignment of responsibility, budgeting, and progress evaluation.

SELF-TEST

Indicate whether each of the following is true or false.

1. _____ Environmental factors that affect marketing decisions are always external and thus are out of the control of the independent consultant.

2. _____ External environmental factors that should be considered when preparing a marketing plan include economic factors, legislation, and cultural and demographic factors.

3. _____ Only the people who are developing the marketing plan and marketing personnel should be aware of the marketing plan.

4. _____ The analogy between a road map and a marketing plan is fictitious rather than real.

5. _____ A marketing plan helps you to determine where you are now, where you want to go, and how to get there.

6. _____ A marketing plan should be simple and short even at the expense of significant details.

7. _____ A marketing plan is an end document and should be regarded as such.

8. _____ As long as your marketing plan is convincing, it really does not matter whether or not it is based on valid assumptions.

9. _____ A marketing plan should be flexible in order to take account of changes in the conditions under which you operate.

10. _____ Market plan targets should be realistic in the sense of being consistent with available resources.

11. _____ It is impossible to know what facts you will need for your marketing plan.

12. _____ The situation analysis should contain information on the size of the market, its growth rate, its demographic features, and pertinent competitive factors.

13. _____ Given the nature of the consulting business, it is impossible for an independent consultant to specify any market segment in the marketing plan.

14. _____ One of the purposes of a marketing plan is to reveal strengths and conceal weaknesses in the business.

15. _____ Preferably, goals should be expressed in concrete numerical terms.

16. _____ The marketing plan should contain an action plan that outlines the strategy that you will use to achieve your marketing objectives.

17. _____ Since marketing is a company-wide activity, there is no need to specify who will be responsible for the implementation of the marketing plan.

18. _____ Budgeting is a separate activity from marketing and therefore has no place in a marketing plan.

19. _____ If financial resources are inadequate to allow for the implementation of the marketing strategy, the marketing plan may have to be modified.

20. _____ A good marketing plan will help you to accomplish your marketing objectives. There is therefore no need for any type of monitoring.

ANSWERS

1. F   2. T   3. F   4. F   5. T   6. F   7. F   8. F

9. T   10. T   11. F   12. T   13. F   14. F   15. T   16. T

17. F   18. F   19. T   20. F

CHAPTER 6
PRICING CONSULTING
SERVICES

INTRODUCTION

In Chapter 3, we saw that price was an important element in the marketing mix. The pricing decision is an important one and should be considered quite seriously. The fee that you charge for your service will partly determine how many clients can afford to pay your fees and how much money you will make as an independent consultant.

We begin this chapter with an investigation into the nature and importance of prices. We then discuss pricing constraints and relate pricing to various objectives. Next, we study some pricing strategies that you may be able to use in your consulting business. Some important psychological aspects of pricing are discussed, with attention given to both consultants (price setters) and clients. We end the module with an examination of various billing methods that merit your consideration.

THE NATURE AND IMPORTANCE OF PRICE

In order to make good pricing decisions, independent consultants must be aware of the nature of price. The price that you charge for your services constitutes your fee. As you already know, price plays an important role in the number and types of clients you attract, and is an important determinant of your income as an independent consultant. In this section, we explore the nature and importance of price.

The Nature of Price

Independent consultants are paid for their services. The price of such services is usually referred to as a fee. Price is often defined as value expressed in terms of money. The fee that your clients are willing to pay is an indication of the value they place on your consulting services. The more valuable your services are to them, the higher is the fee (price) that they will be willing to pay.

Most people would define price as the amount of money a buyer pays to obtain a good or a service from a seller. Expressed in different terms, we may say that price is the monetary value of goods and services that are traded in the market place. This layman's definition of price is important because it is easy to understand, and it reflects the clients' perception.

Often in business, what the clients think is more important than what the experts think. However, it is not your clients who make decisions about pricing. If they did, you would not have any clients to serve you would not be in business for very long. Most clients do not see any difference between *price* and *cost*. As far as a client is concerned, if she pays $250 for a particular service, she will say that the service costs her $250. And that's O.K. for her, but it may not be O.K. for you. One of the first things that you need to realize about price is that it is different from cost, and the difference is crucial. Technically, price refers to selling price, whereas cost refers to the cost of offering the service.

As an independent consultant, it is important to understand how people tend to view price. People tend to judge the quality of a product by its price. In their perception, the higher the price, the greater the quality. This is one of the many factors that the independent consultant must keep in mind when deciding on a fee.

The Importance of Pricing

Price plays an important role in influencing the purchasing decisions of consumers. Most consumers (your clients and prospective clients) are interested in value. Actually, value can be defined as the ratio of perceived benefits to price. Symbolically:

$$\textbf{V = B/P,} \text{ where}$$
$$V = \text{value}$$
$$B = \text{perceived benefits}$$
$$P = \text{price}$$

For example, if clients evaluate the perceived benefit from a service as $200.00 and the price of the service is $100.00, then the value will be (200 ÷ 100) = $2.00. If the price were $50.00 instead of $100.00, then the value would be (200 ÷ 50) = $4.00. Clearly, a low price associated with large benefits translates into high value.

Moreover, the above relationship between value, perceived benefits, and price means that value can be increased either by lowering price or by increasing perceived benefits.

This chapter is based on the assumption that the objective of your consulting business is to make as much profit as possible, given the business environment. However, acknowledging the possibility of other objectives, we consider the role of pricing in the profit as well as in other objectives. We assume that care has been taken to minimize cost. We assume that adequate marketing has taken place and that other preconditions of profitability, such as excellent service and a trained staff have been attended to. Without these other *profit essentials*, you will not maximize your profit, no matter how efficient you may be in pricing your consulting service.

To see just how important pricing is, let us look at what we call the *profit function*. Don't let this technical term bother you. The profit function simply means the factors that determine profits. There are basically three factors that determine profits:

> price
> cost
> volume

Price, as we have indicated earlier, is what you charge your clients for your services, the cost is what you incur to provide the services, and the volume is the quantity that you will sell, that is, how many assignments you will get or how many clients will call upon you to provide services. It is well known that the fee that you charge will affect the quantity that you sell (the number of clients you serve). In general, if you lower you fee, you will attract more clients. However, that does not mean that you will make more profits.

We need to look more closely at profits. Profit is the difference between your total revenue and your total cost. We can write a formula for profits as follows:

Profit = TR - TC

Don't let this formula scare you. It is actually very simple and quite easy to understand. TR is total revenue, and TC is total cost. The formula says that if you bill 100 clients $50 each, then your total revenue is $5,000. Now, if you incurred a cost of $3,500 to provide the services, then your profit would be $5000 - 3500 = $1500. We can see the importance of price.

Suppose you had charged a fee of $40 instead of $50. At this lower price, the number of clients will increase. If the number increases to 150 clients, then your total revenue will be (150 x $40) = $6000. If the cost incurred increased from $3500 to $4200, your total profits would now climb to $6000 - $4200 = $1800. This simple example illustrates two important facts:

1. *You may be able to increase your profit simply by changing your price.*
2. *A lower price does not necessarily mean less profits.*

The fee that you charge for your consulting services is one of the most strategic elements in the ultimate success or failure of your consulting practice. It makes good sense to know how to set your fees in a manner that will contribute to the accomplishment of your objective.

PRICING CONSTRAINTS AND OBJECTIVES

Your pricing decisions will be governed by two main forces — several pricing constraints and the objectives that you want your pricing decisions to accomplish. Let us turn our attention to these two forces.

Pricing Constraints

There will be many factors that limit your flexibility in terms of fee setting. These limiting factors are referred to as *pricing constraints*. Pricing constraints include factors such as:

- demand for your service
- competitors' fees
- cost of providing the service
- nature of your market

Let us now briefly discuss each of these pricing constraints.

Demand for Your Service

Clearly, the number of clients and potential clients who want to use your consulting service will affect the fee that you can charge. The perception that clients and potential clients have of your service, for example, whether they consider it a luxury or a necessity, will also affect the fee that you can charge.

Competitors Fees

The fee that you can set for your services depends, to a large extent, on the fees that your competitors charge for similar services. If a competitor whose services are considered to be similar to yours charges $75 an hour, it is unlikely that you will be able to charge $150 an hour and attract clients.

Cost of Providing the Service

If you consistently charge a fee that does not cover the cost of providing the service, you won't have to worry about pricing because in the long run, you will not have a consulting practice. Remember that the cost of providing the service includes the cost of marketing the service, and the cost of your time. Your cost then, sets the lower limit of your fee.

Nature of Your Market

The market structure in which you operate limits your flexibility in terms of setting your fees. Economists discuss market competitiveness in terms of four types of market structures:

- pure competition
- monopolistic competition
- oligopoly
- monopoly

Pure Competition is a market structure in which numerous sellers are offering similar products for sale. *Monopolistic competition* is a market structure in which many sellers offer differentiated products for sale. The products are considered to be close substitutes. An *oligopoly* is a market structure in which there are few sellers whose actions are interdependent. A *monopoly* is a market structure in which there is only one seller of the product. Clearly, if your clients have a choice of selecting from several independent consultants, your flexibility in setting your fee is significantly different from the case where you are the only consultant available.

Pricing Objectives

The term *pricing objectives* refers to the goals that your pricing strategy is aimed at accomplishing. Among the goals that you may pursue are:

- profit
- sales
- market share
- client value
- staying alive

Let us discuss each of these objectives briefly.

Profit

You may have as your objective, profit maximization in the short run, or profit maximization in the long run. Alternatively, you may set a satisfactory level of profit as your objective instead of profit maximization.

Sales (Revenue)

If you consider that your current profit level is satisfactory, you may consider an increase in revenue as an objective. In general, the fee that will lead to maximum profit is different from that which will maximize sales revenue. It is possible however, for an increase in sales revenue to lead to an increase in profit.

Market Share

Market share refers to the ratio of your sales revenues to the total revenues of the industry. Of course, the industry is defined in terms of your field. Thus, if you are an educational consultant, then your industry will be the educational consulting industry. Market share represents the fraction of the total market that you serve. Although an increase in market share may be an end in itself, it is often a means to some other end such as increased sales revenue or increased profits.

Client Value

Many independent consultants base their marketing strategy on client value. They claim that providing value to their clients is an important marketing objective. Recall that value is the ratio of perceived benefits to price.

Staying Alive

Many independent consultants find themselves in a situation where the survival of their practice is seriously threatened. In such circumstances, other pricing objectives diminish in importance when compared with the survival objective.

PRICING STRATEGIES

Before we discuss pricing strategies, perhaps it's a good idea for us to explain what we mean by a strategy. If you have been a consultant for any length of time, it is very likely that you have had to use some kind of strategy. Probably you have had to use resources to carry out some activity in response to an action that may have been taken by one or more of your competitors. We can define a strategy as the utilization or deployment of resources to accomplish established objectives in response to active opposition. Pricing is an important selling and marketing strategy.

A variety of pricing strategies are available to independent consultants. Some of these strategies are:

- penetration pricing
- cost plus pricing
- prestige pricing
- competitor lead pricing
- target return pricing

Penetration Pricing

Independent consultants who are just entering the consulting business may consider using penetration pricing. This pricing strategy involves setting a low fee initially in order to attract clients. Penetration pricing will tend to be effective when the consultant's clients and potential clients are price-sensitive.

If you decide to use penetration pricing, you need to consider its disadvantages. First, once you have established a low fee, it may be difficult to increase it at a later stage. Second, a low-price strategy may give the impression of low quality of service, since many people tend to judge quality by price. Third, a low fee might bring in more clients than you can serve efficiently. Finally, penetration pricing means that you will have to spend more of your time in order to earn a given amount of money. This, of course, is an important consideration for independent consultants.

Cost-Plus Pricing

Cost plus pricing is certainly the simplest and probably the most popular pricing technique used by independent consultants. A markup on cost is quite common. In some cases, the percentage added to costs is based on industry tradition, but in many cases, it is determined by the judgment of the independent consultant.

The popularity of this strategy is due partly to the fact that many of those who use it regard prices that cover costs as providing them with some notion of a fair profit. As far as the consumer is concerned, setting prices in this way may have very little to do with fairness.

Problems with Cost Plus Pricing

Perhaps you are among the many independent consultants who use cost plus pricing, and perhaps you are quite satisfied with it because it is relatively easy to use and understand. You may have been making profits using this technique. But the real question is, are you achieving your pricing objectives?

One problem with cost-plus pricing is that it does not take client demand sufficiently into consideration. Let us be realistic. A price that is determined simply by adding an arbitrarily established markup to costs is somewhat like a "hit or miss" device. The result may be a price that is either too high or too low in terms of helping you to achieve your objectives. A pricing strategy that has a profit objective, for example, should take into account consumer needs, ability, and willingness to pay.

Another problem with this strategy is that it is often difficult to determine costs accurately. The problem arises mainly because of the difficulty of allocating overhead expenses to specific consulting assignments.

Yet another difficulty with cost-plus pricing is that it does not take into account the activities of your competitors and the fees that they charge. If the services of other consultants are considered to be good alternatives (substitutes) for your service, you cannot afford to ignore their fees.

Prestige Pricing

Based on the premise that clients tend to equate a high price with high quality, you may use a high-price strategy to convey the idea of high quality and prestige. Prestige pricing involves setting a high fee to attract certain types of clients. The "you get what you pay for" idea is behind the prestige pricing strategy. Prestige pricing will tend to be effective when your clients and prospective clients are status-conscious.

Once you have chosen prestige pricing, you are in fact announcing to the world that you are a high-quality consultant who is worthy of your fee. The onus is then on you to live up to your advertisement. If you can justify high fees by the quality of your service, your clients will pay. If you can use this method of pricing, you will be able to isolate yourself somewhat from the vagaries of price competition. A low price is relatively easy to copy, but it is a much more difficult task to imitate competition that is based on such intangible elements as high-quality service, credibility, and reputation.

Competitor-Lead Pricing

New independent consultants who are unsure of how to establish their fees may simply follow the lead of their competitors. If you decide to use this method of setting your fee, you must remember that your costs may be different from those of your competitors. So too, you must consider that you are unlikely to attract many clients unless you can convince them that there are additional benefits to be derived from using your service. Such benefits may include easy access to consultation, quick service delivered on schedule, and perhaps a pick-up and delivery service, depending on your area of consulting.

Target-Return Pricing

There is no justification for the existence of a consulting business if it does not earn a return on the investment in it. Target return pricing involves setting a profit target, and then striving to attain the target. You could, for example, establish a rate of return of 15 percent on your investment, and then set out to earn that target. Don't forget to include the cost of your time as a part of your investment in your practice.

How do you decide on the rate of profit that you should set as the target? This can only be arbitrary. Your rate of profit depends on a wide variety of factors, including, but not limited to the following:

- the nature of your consulting business
- the degree of competition
- the size of your market (potential clients)
- your geographic location
- your marketing skills.

In any event, if you use this strategy, the target rate of return should never be set below the prevailing rate of interest.

Drawbacks of Target Return Pricing

One of the problems associated with target return pricing is that, like cost plus pricing, it is not market-oriented. It does not place sufficient emphasis on the client. Another difficulty with this strategy is that its success depends heavily on the accuracy of the revenue forecast. If the revenue forecast is incorrect, the target return will not be accomplished.

PSYCHOLOGICAL ASPECTS OF PRICING

We have known for decades now that purely psychological factors play an important role in clients' buying behavior. Many clients seem to be motivated by factors other than the fees that consultants charge. Some of the nonfee factors that clients consider include:

- the reputation of the consultant
- the consultant's credibility

- friendly and pleasant disposition
- company image

Moreover, many (if not most) consultants base their pricing decisions on assumptions about their clients' behavior, most of which are psychological in nature. It follows then, that to make successful pricing decisions, the consultant must be familiar with certain psychological elements related to pricing.

Psychology of Price Setters (Consultants)

It is an undisputed fact that typical independent consultants, when setting their fees, are very much concerned with such factors as costs, fees charged by their competitors, and the possible reaction of their clients to their fees and to those of their competitors. It would be surprising if you did not fall into this category. And that is quite natural. After all, you obtain your income from fees so you pay a great deal of attention to fees, and we have stressed the significance of pricing for the success of your consulting practice. But we must also consider how our clients view prices (fees). We cannot afford to have a distorted image of the importance of fees *from the client's point of view*.

We now have rather convincing evidence that most clients are not as sensitive to fees as most independent consultants assume. (Next time you get the opportunity, take a good look at the prices that many people are willing to pay for certain types of running shoes. Although you are not selling running shoes, the information should tell you something.) Since it is known that most clients do not really react to small differences in fees, it has been suggested by some experts that because of their psychological involvement with fees, independent consultants may be systematically charging less than would be consistent with their desire to increase their income.

There is another psychological block that impairs the ability of some independent consultants to make efficient pricing decisions: the obsession with basing prices on cost. We mentioned this tendency earlier, but let us discuss it again here. Several scientific studies have concluded that the most commonly used method of calculating a fee is to maintain a constant difference between some concept of cost and the price (fee). This is the strategy of *cost-plus pricing* that we discussed earlier in this chapter. As we mentioned earlier, this pricing strategy ignores demand considerations and may lead to some irrational pricing decisions.

When there is a general price level increase in the economy, many independent consultants maintain their established fees since they do not see themselves purchasing inputs, with the possible exception of labor services, at higher prices. Following the same logic, when their expenses go up, they try to pass all the increases on to their clients, regardless of whether or not such a decision is justified by demand considerations.

Sometimes, past training can affect independent consultants in rather subtle ways. Consider the backgrounds of most independent consultants. Most of them have a strong technical background. By virtue of this conditioning, they tend to view things from a particular perspective. As a result, their judgment in setting prices may be biased in many ways.

To the extent that they are aware of costs, independent consultants with technical backgrounds, such as chemistry, engineering, computer technology, gardening, or construction, tend to be extremely cost-conscious. Such consultants tend to price their services to cover full accounting costs. Their actions will often be influenced by the expectations and norms of their peer groups, that is professionals with whom they identify because of a similarity in background. They also tend to be inflexible toward any fee adjustments.

On the other hand, independent consultants with a sales background tend to underestimate costs and to overestimate demand factors. Because their primary orientation is toward volume rather than profits, their immediate impulse is to lower their fees to increase their clientele. Many former salespeople who venture into independent consulting fail to earn an adequate return on their investment in money, time, and effort because of an unduly low fee policy.

Psychology of Clients

We have looked at the psychological aspects of price setting by independent consultants, and we have seen that they often use cost-plus pricing which does not necessarily result in the accomplishment of pricing objectives. Now we shall look at the psychology of the clients.

Clients usually perceive fees in a noneconomic manner. Value is the main factor that they take into consideration when buying consulting services. Recall our discussion of value earlier in this chapter. Therefore, creating a sense of value should be one of the goals toward which pricing policy strives. Remember that clients tend to associate high fees with good quality. There are some interesting cases in which clients have decided not to engage the services of independent consultants because their fees were too low.

The foregoing should not be interpreted as a refutation of the idea that many clients are price-conscious. If clients were not price-conscious, then pricing would not have the effect on income that it does. Clients are price conscious, but price is not the only significant factor to clients. It is a fact that many clients are willing to pay higher fees. Why? That is what we will investigate in the next section.

Why Are Clients Willing to Pay Higher Fees?

You know from your own experience that the lower-priced product is not always the biggest seller. Why is this so? Three main factors provide the answer to this question:

- client ignorance
- snob appeal
- perceived risk

Let us now consider each of these factors in turn.

Consumer Ignorance

We have been told repeatedly that the average modern consumer is well-informed. To a certain extent, this is true. But how many clients are experts in your field?

The fact is, most of your clients are unable to judge the quality of your service until after they have purchased it. Faced with this problem, many clients try to evaluate the quality of consulting services by such yardsticks as price, the consultant's reputation, and the appearance of the consultant's office. Many independent consultants have managed to run successful consulting practices by creating an image of being more prestigious and more expensive.

Snob Appeal

Over 100 years ago, Thorstein Veblen, in his book, *The Theory of the Leisure Class*, described the concept of "conspicuous consumption." Many people prefer to pay high prices because of snobbishness. The same is true of consulting services. Many clients receive a certain amount of satisfaction from being able to say that they engage the services of some high price, prestigious consultant.

Perceived Risk

Another reason that clients are willing to pay more for consulting services is the perceived risk that they associate with the spending. Clients may prefer to pay more for a particular service and be assured of reliable quality. This reduces risk and anxiety. The additional fee is considered by many clients to be well worth it, because it provides them with peace of mind.

WAYS OF BILLING

Once you have decided the fee that you will charge for your services, you need to consider the method of billing that you will use. For example, some professionals bill on an hourly basis while some bill on a "per visit" basis. Independent consultants have five choices:

1. billing on an hourly basis
2. billing on a daily basis
3. billing on a performance basis
4. billing on a fixed fee basis
5. billing on a retainer basis

Let us discuss each of these ways of billing.

Billing On An Hourly Basis

Hourly rate billing is quite common among independent consultants. An experienced consultant may, after experimenting for a few years, decide that an hourly rate of $75 is an appropriate fee. But new consultants would want to know how to arrive at an hourly rate.

Let us assume that just before you became an independent consultant, you earned $50,000 a year from an employer. Let us assume also that other employment benefits add up to $10,000 a year, making a total of $60,000 a year. Let us assume further that you worked 40 hours a week for 48 weeks a year. This means that you worked for a total of 1,920 hours a year. So your hourly rate was $60,000 ☐ 1,920 = $31.25. If you figure that in order to earn $60,000 you must charge $31.25 an hour, you are making a big mistake.

Let's see why.

Suppose that your expenses for the year as an independent consultant are as shown in Table 6.1 below.

If you want to receive an annual income of $60,000, you must bill for $60,000 + $42,000 = $102,200. Assuming that the total number of hours remains at 1,920, your hourly rate will be $53.23. So if you set your fee at $54 an hour, you will cover your annual income of $60,000.

Table 6.1. Calculation of Hourly Rate

Rent	$ 6,000
Telephone	2,000
Transportation	2,500
Insurance	3,000
Advertising, etc.	10,000
Administrative and legal	5,000
Secretarial and clerical	7,000
Office equipment	1,500
Office supplies	500
Professional dues	1,500
Entertainment	2,500
Postage	200
Miscellaneous	2,000
Total	**42,200**

Remember, however, that the calculation is based on the assumption that you do work 40 hours a week. Therefore, in order to meet your $60,000 a year income objective, you must have enough work to keep you busy for 1,920 hours a year. If you work fewer hours, your annual income will be less than $60,000 unless you change your hourly rate. Consultants often have more than one project going at a time, so hourly rate billing turns out to be convenient. You simply log the number of hours you work on each client's assignment.

Billing On A Daily Basis

Instead of billing on an hourly basis, you could decide to bill on a daily basis. The calculation of a daily rate is similar to that involved in arriving at an hourly rate. You figure out the number of days per year that you will work (N), the annual income you require (I), and your annual expenses (E). Then you add I and E together, and then divide the result by N. You can use the following formula to calculate your daily rate.

$$DR = \frac{I + E}{N}$$

Where   DR = daily rate
I = annual income required
E = annual expenses
N = number of working days per year

Obviously, daily rate billing may not be as flexible as hourly rate billing. However, billing on a daily basis may be convenient for many independent consultants. If, for example, you accept an assignment that requires your presence at your client's organization for four full days, then daily rate billing might be an option to consider.

Billing On A Performance Basis

Billing on a performance basis is similar to being paid on a commission basis. Your fee is tied to your performance. Suppose you are a marketing consultant. You could arrange a fee of 15 percent of increased sales resulting from your recommendations. If you decide to use this method of billing, make sure that the terms of engagement are clearly spelled out *in writing.*

One advantage of performance billing is that it has the potential to inspire confidence. The client could reason that the consultant must be sure of success in making such an arrangement. Another advantage of performance billing is that it involves little or no risk to the client since there is no cost without results. Clearly these two advantages make billing on a performance basis a powerful marketing technique.

A caveat is in order here. If you decide to bill on a performance basis, you must be relatively sure that you can get the job done, or you must have other assignments that are reliable sources of income. If you are not too busy with other engagements, you may consider using the performance billing arrangement.

Billing On A Fixed-Fee Basis

Billing on a fixed fee basis involves charging a fixed fee for an assignment. Whether you take a few hours or a few days or a few weeks to complete the assignment, your fee is the same. If you choose to bill on a fixed fee basis, it is to your advantage to complete the assignment as quickly as possible.

It is probably a good idea not to use fixed fee billing unless you are quite sure of the amount of time that you will require to complete the assignment. New and inexperienced independent consultants sometimes use fixed fee billing to their detriment. The underestimate the time required to complete the assignment and the expenses that they will incur, thus ending up getting little or no money for a considerable amount of work.

Even experienced independent consultants need to be careful with billing on a fixed fee basis. If an experienced consultant who has prepared many organizational manuals is asked to prepare an Organization Manual for an organization with which he/she is quite familiar, he/she could opt for a fixed fee arrangement. But the unknown presents an element of risk, so even in such a case, an amount should be included in your fee to cover the unknown element.

Since many clients are known to insist on being billed on a fixed fee basis, it is important to have some kind of formula that can be used as a guide in arriving at your fee. The following example may be helpful. You receive an assignment and you estimate that it will take you ten days to complete it. Other estimates of time and cost are included in the following Table 6.2. The estimates contain a reasonable allowance for the unknown factor.

Table 6.2. Calculation of Fixed Fee

Labor Costs:

Consultant 10 days at $600 a day =	$6,000	
Secretarial 10 days at $ 80 a day =	$ 800	
Total labor cost		**$6,800**

Expenses:

Hotel	$ 150	
Air fare	$ 350	
Printing and binding	$ 150	
Miscellaneous expenses	$ 50	
Total expenses		**$ 700**

Overhead (55 % of labor cost)	**$ 3,740**
TOTAL FEE	**$11,240**

Some consultants, especially if they are incorporated, add a certain percentage profit on the total fee and then bill accordingly. For example, if you consider that a profit of 10 percent is reasonable, then you will bill for a total fee of $11,240 + $1,124 = $12,364.

Billing On A Retainer Basis

Most reputable independent consultants are quite busy. This means that if clients require their services at any particular time, they can oblige only by giving up work on some other assignment. Many clients need consultation frequently only for a few minutes. But these few minutes represent intrusions on the consultant's time. Moreover, many clients like to know that their consultants will be available to them when needed. Thus, working on a retainer basis can be mutually beneficial to both the consultant and the client.

Billing on a retainer basis means that you receive a constant monthly fee in exchange for the insurance of a certain amount of your time to the client, whether or not the time is used. The guarantee that you will be available to your client on a priority basis is considered to be a fair trade off for the constant monthly fee. Many clients will attempt to treat consultants on a retainer as if they are employees. But you must remember that you are an independent consultant and that the constant monthly fee that is paid by your clients does not, in any way, change your status to that of an employee.

CHAPTER SUMMARY

1. Price may be defined as value expressed in terms of money. A direct relationship exists between the value your clients place on your services and the fee that they will be willing to pay.

2. The difference between price and cost is that price is what the user pays for the product (good or service) while the cost is the amount the seller incurs in order to offer the product for sale.

3. Because price and value are so closely related, and because clients are value conscious, it is important for independent consultants to understand price. Price, cost and volume determine profits.

4. Pricing constraints are the factors that limit one's flexibility in terms of fee setting. They include demand, competitors' fees, cost, and the nature of the market.

5. Pricing objectives are the goals that pricing strategy is trying to achieve. They may include profit, revenues, market share, client value, and staying alive (survival).

6. Independent consultants have a variety of pricing strategies, including penetration pricing, cost plus pricing, prestige pricing, competitor lead pricing, and target return pricing.

7. An effective pricing strategy requires the price setter to take certain psychological aspects of pricing into consideration.

8. Independent consultants may choose from a variety of billing methods, including hourly basis, daily basis, performance basis, fixed fee basis, and retainer basis.

SELF-TEST QUESTIONS

Indicate whether each of the following is true (T) or false (F)

1. _____ Independent consulting services are not traded in any market, therefore the consultant's fee is not really a price.

2. _____ Independent consultants don't have to be concerned about pricing decisions since it is their clients who determine what the price of their services will be.

3. _____ The terms "price" and "cost" can always be used interchangeably because the two concepts are identical.

4. _____ When deciding on a fee, the independent consultant must keep in mind that clients tend to associate quality with price.

5. _____ The value of consulting services can be increased either by increasing perceived benefits or by lowering the price of the services.

6. _____ The importance of good pricing decisions can be gauged from the fact that even in the absence of other factors that contribute to profits, independent consultants can still maximize profits by efficient pricing decisions alone.

7. _____ Profit is determined mainly by price, cost, and volume.

8. _____ Independent consultants cam always increase their profits by lowering their fees, and thus increase the number of clients they serve.

9. _____ If a consultant lowers his/her fee, his/her profits will necessarily decline.

10. ____ One of the great advantages that independent consultants enjoy is that there are no limits to their flexibility in terms of fee setting.

11. ____ Pricing constraints include factors such as competitors' fees, cost of providing the service, and the degree of competition in the market.

12. ____ If you are the only consultant in town, you will have more control over the price that you can charge than if there are several other consultants in town.

13. ____ All consultants try to set a price for their services that will generate maximum profits.

14. ____ If your price leads to maximum revenue, then it will also generate maximum profits.

15. ____ Penetration pricing will tend to be effective when clients and prospective clients are price conscious.

16. ____ One possible effect of penetration pricing is that the consultant who uses it may have to spend more of his/her time in order to earn a given amount of money.

17. _____ One important advantage of cost-plus pricing is that it takes the activities of the consultant's competitors into consideration.

18. _____ Cost-plus pricing is quite popular among independent consultants because it is most likely to result in profit maximization.

19. _____ In general, lower fees attract more clients, but a high fee may attract certain types of clients.

20. _____ Qualities such as credibility and reputation are much more difficult to imitate than low prices.

21. _____ A safe way to set your fee is to follow the lead of your competitors.

22. _____ There are clear and precise guidelines for determining the rate of profit that a consultant should establish as a target.

23. _____ Target-return pricing is not market oriented.

24. _____ Clients' buying behaviour depends solely on economic and financial factors.

25. _____ In order to make successful pricing decisions, consultants must be familiar with certain psychological elements related to pricing.

26. _____ Most clients are extremely price conscious, therefore, in order to formulate an effective pricing strategy, the consultant should try to keep his/her price as low as possible in order to earn as much income as possible.

27. _____ It is a very smart pricing strategy to raise your fees whenever your costs increase.

28. ____ When purchasing consulting services, the main factors that clients take into consideration is the consultant's fee.

29. ____ One of the goals toward which pricing policy should strive is creating a sense of value.

30. ____ Some independent consultants have lost consulting engagements because their fees were too low.

31. ____ Consumer ignorance has no significance in modern pricing because the modern consumer is well informed.

32. ____ Perceived risk may explain why some clients prefer to pay a higher price for consulting services.

33. ____ Hourly-rate billing is not popular among independent consultants because they always prefer to bill on a fixed-fee basis.

34. ____ It a consultant wants to earn an annual income of $50,000, he/she should bill clients for $50,000.

35. ____ Consultants who have more than one project going at a time may find hourly-rate billing to be convenient.

36. ____ In calculating a daily rate, the consultant should not consider the number of working days per year.

37. _____ An independent consultant should avoid billing on a performance basis unless he/she is relatively sure that he/she can get the job done.

38. _____ The best time to use performance billing is when you are extremely busy with other engagements.

39. _____ A consultant who uses fixed-fee billing could end up getting little or no money for a considerable amount of work.

40. _____ Fixed-fee billing presents a problem only for new and inexperienced consultants.

41. _____ In fixed-fee billing, it is unethical to include an amount to account for unknown factors because the client should not be expected to pay for such unknown factors.

42. _____ A reputable independent consultant who is usually very busy should never accept work on a retainer basis.

43. _____ An independent consultant who receives a regular monthly fee on a retainer basis has effectively become an employee of the client who retains his/her services.

44. _____ Working on a retainer basis can be beneficial to both consultant and client.

45. _____ Although there is a difference between price and cost, the difference is not really crucial. After all, price is derived from cost.

46. _____ Many clients believe that price and quality are directly related. That is, the higher the price, the better the quality.

47. _____ Pure competition is a market structure in which there are only a few firms competing fiercely for market share.

48. _____ Prestige pricing sends out a message that clients can expect a high quality of service.

49. _____ The success of target-return pricing has little or nothing to do with the accuracy of the revenue forecast.

50. _____ Clients are not at all price conscious, so independent consultants need not worry about clients' ability to pay.

ANSWERS

1. F	2. F	3. F	4. T	5. T	6. F	7. T	8. F
9. F	10. F	11. T	12. T	13. F	14. F	15. T	16. T
17. F	18. F	19. T	20. T	21. F	22. F	23. T	24. F
25. T	26. F	27. F	28. F	29. T	30. T	31. F	32. T
33. F	34. F	35. T	36. F	37. T	38. F	39. T	40. F
41. F	42. F	43. F	44. T	45. F	46. T	47. F	48. T
49. F	50. F						

CHAPTER 7
PROPOSAL WRITING

INTRODUCTION

Every independent consultant will write several proposals in the course of his/her consulting career. Clients will ask for them, and consultants will probably submit some even though they may not be requested. It is not an exaggeration to say that the success of your consulting practice depends, to a great extent, on the quality of proposals that you write. If you cannot produce winning proposals, you will lose many consulting assignments to your competitors who can.

In this chapter, our attention will be focused on an extremely important aspect of independent consulting: proposal writing. We begin the discussion by defining the term "proposal" and then proceed to explain why consultants write proposals. Next, we discuss the objectives of proposals and then examine the main parts and format of a proposal. We end the chapter with an example of a short proposal.

PROPOSAL WRITING

There are good writers and there are poor writers. The consultant who does not have good writing skills is at a distinct disadvantage in the race for consulting work. If you do not possess adequate skills in written communication, then you should definitely have a qualified individual look over your proposals before they are submitted. Knowing how to write winning proposals contributes to the success of your consulting practice. This section of the module will illustrate how you can transmit the information necessary to demonstrate credibility, confidence, capability and competence in your proposals.

PROPOSAL DEFINED

An important step in writing effective proposals is to recognize that a proposal is a sales document. Whatever else it may do, its main objective is to influence the prospective client to use your consulting services. We can define a proposal as a document that outlines a plan of action to be followed in executing an assignment or an engagement. The consultant needs to understand that the proposal should detail *what* he/she intends to do not *how* it will be done. If your proposal details how the assignment will be done, then there is no need for the client to engage your services.

The consulting proposal must spell out the benefits that the prospective client will derive from accepting your proposal. Let us assume that your prospective client is a business organization. Your proposal must demonstrate convincingly that you have the capability to do the following:

1. assist the organization to accomplish established goals
2. contribute to the organization's productivity
3. help the organization become more efficient and more effective
4. help the organization to save time and money
5. complete assignments with excellence and on schedule.

Your proposals must perform this function otherwise, you are simply wasting your time by preparing them and submitting them for consideration. Your clients are looking for help. If your proposal does not convey the message that you can offer help, what reason is there for the client to engage your services? None.

WHY PROPOSE?

Why is it necessary for an independent consultant to prepare and submit a written proposal? There are many reasons for writing proposals and we discuss some of them here.

1. They are requested by clients

Modern life, whether personal or business, has become quite complex. We live in a high-tech age, and decision-making has become a rather complicated process. More information is needed and greater objectivity is required. Clients are value-conscious and they want to be assured that they are getting good value for a given budget.

Clients are demanding to know what quality of service they can expect for their money. Will they be getting their money's worth from their purchasing decisions? The written proposal is intended to answer this question.

2. They assist in securing work

You cannot win a lottery if you don't have a ticket. You cannot win a race if you don't compete. In many instances, you cannot get the assignment unless you submit a written proposal. The written proposal is a marketing tool that you can use to "sell" your consulting services to potential clients.

3. They are being written by your competitors

Another reason for writing proposals is that your competitors are busy doing it. Independent consultants are submitting proposals, both solicited and unsolicited. Many are taking the initiative of using written proposals to direct clients' attention to the existence of a need, and to convince prospective clients to use their services to satisfy that need. If you do not get on board, you will be left behind.

4. They prepare you for the actual assignment

The entire process of preparing a proposal document can be viewed as preparation for the actual consulting work that will be done if the consultant obtains the assignment. The actual work will flow much more smoothly just because a proposal was prepared in advance of the performance of the actual work.

5. They provide guidelines for performance

The existence of a written proposal can be used as a guideline for executing the task to be performed. In fact, the consultant will find it useful to refer to the proposal many times during the performance of the engagement. For example, by consulting the proposal document, the consultant can determine whether or not the work is progressing on schedule.

6. They convey important information

A written document outlining the work to be performed, the time frame in which the work will be performed, and the fee to be paid is of great value both to the consultant and the client. The client knows exactly what to expect, and the consultant knows exactly what to deliver.

PROPOSAL OBJECTIVES

The independent consultant must understand and totally accept the fact that the proposal document is an important marketing tool. Like the sales letter discussed in Chapter 3, the proposal document should exemplify the AIDA approach. It should:

> - attract the prospect's **a**ttention
> - arouse his/her **i**nterest
> - create a **d**esire
> - stimulate **a**ction.

The ultimate objective of the proposal document is to bring the prospective client to the point where he/she decides to engage your services. This is accomplished by convincing the prospective client that:

1. the solution you propose to offer is the best one available to solve his/her problem

2. you are the most qualified and in the best position to perform the assignment

3. you have made provisions to allocate the necessary resources to perform the assignment effectively and efficiently

4. the proposed fee is quite reasonable and that the value he/she will receive is substantial.

Specific sections of the proposal document should convey the above information.

Since one of the main objectives of the proposal document is to convincingly demonstrate your ability to deliver work of the highest quality, it follows that the proposal document itself should be of the highest quality. A fact that is too often overlooked is that the quality of the proposal provides an indication of the quality of work that the client can expect from the consultant. You should use your proposal to portray an image of professionalism and to convey the impression that your consulting enterprise takes great pride in its work. The proposal document should be of high quality both in content and appearance. Excellent appearance and poor content do not make winning proposals.

THE MAIN PARTS OF A PROPOSAL

A proposal has the following three main parts:

1. The technical section

2. The organization and management section

3. The cost section.

This section of the chapter discusses each of these parts in some detail.

The Technical Section

The technical section is the most important part of the proposal. In this section, the consultant states the details of the work to be performed, the methodology that will be used, and the time for the completion of each phase. This section of the proposal should:

1. Show that you understand the nature of the client's problem and that you fully understand the work that is to be done.

2. Demonstrate your competence and expertise in the field in which the proposed engagement falls. For example, if the proposed project falls within the field of education, you should show that you have qualifications in that field and that you have *successfully* undertaken similar projects.

3. Give the client the assurance that the work will be performed according to specifications and to the client's satisfaction.

These requirements can be met by:

1. Providing a detailed description of the work to be done.

2. Providing a detailed description of the means by which the work will be performed.

Let us consider each of these elements.

Work Description

Remember that your proposal will be submitted to your prospective client for evaluation. Therefore, the description of the proposed work should be lucid, readable, and written in a manner that facilitates evaluation. The words, sentences, and paragraphs describing the work to be performed can have a greater impact if they are accompanied by diagrams, schedules, and charts. These devices are particularly helpful in the presentation of technical data. In this section we shall discuss the following presentation aids:

1. sketches and drawings
2. photographs
3. schematics and flow diagrams

Sketches and Drawings: It is not advisable to use rough sketches in a proposal unless the purpose is to draw attention to the originality of the concept being presented. Computer-generated designs may be included for special effects. Depending on the nature of the proposed work, sketches and drawings may be an essential part of the presentation. For example, engineers and architects may find drawings to be an essential part of their proposals.

Photographs: True photographs can be very convincing. They may be used when describing items such as equipment, tools, or layouts that are relevant to the proposed work. Credibility is enhanced when photographs are used to show what the end product of an engagement will look like. The consultant should try to limit the number of photographs used in the proposal document.

Schematics and Diagrams: Schematics and flow diagrams can be used effectively to illustrate certain aspects of the proposal. You may be able to take advantage of color in schematics and flow diagrams for comparison and contrast. You must remember that the purpose of this exercise is to provide information and not merely to impress the prospective client. Therefore, schematics and diagrams used in the technical part of the proposal should be simple and straightforward. Complicated diagrams that are difficult to understand may do more harm than good, as they may detract from the information that you are trying to provide.

Description of the Means by Which the Work Will Be Performed

(Note: Some consultants prefer to discuss this aspect of the proposal in the organization and management section of the proposal.)

A description of the means of accomplishing the proposed task should be a part of the proposal. It reflects that the consultant has done some planning and scheduling. This section of the proposal provides you with an opportunity to demonstrate to the prospective client that you are competent to perform the proposed assignment efficiently   with an economic utilization of resources, and with minimum delays.

If possible, the time allotted to the completion of each phase of the project as well as the proposed steps to be taken should be indicated.   If interim reports are expected, the timing of their release should be indicated, and the completion date along with the date for submitting the final report should be included in this part of the proposal.

Establishing the time that it will take to complete each phase of an assignment requires good judgment. The consultant must make this decision, keeping in mind the availability of material and human resources required to perform the task. In establishing the time schedule, it is a good idea to make allowance for unforeseen contingencies. In many instances, time can be saved by scheduling certain activities simultaneously and by permitting overlapping activities.

Most consulting engagements involve a series of steps. It is in the technical section of the proposal that these steps are outlined. Depending on the nature of the assignment, the steps may include:

- ➢ project planning
- ➢ development of appropriate tools
- ➢ data collection
- ➢ interviewing
- ➢ data recording
- ➢ data analysis and computations
- ➢ general report preparation
- ➢ monitoring and follow-up reports

Consultant Client Interaction

All consulting assignments involve some kind of interaction between the consultant and the client. In some situations, the client may be a private individual with whom the consultant interacts on a one-to-one basis. An example of this type of one-to-one interaction is that between a bridal consultant and the future bride. In other situations, the client may be a business organization. In this case, the assignment might involve all employees of the organization, or it might involve only a few people, such as upper management personnel. The consultant may find it advisable to indicate in this section of the proposal the degree and level of client involvement. For example, the client would appreciate knowing whether the consultant will hold interviews with management and staff, and the frequency of such interviews.

The Organization and Management Section

In this section of the proposal, the consultant should outline how resources will be organized and managed in order to accomplish the proposed activity. If certain members of the consulting team will be assigned specific functions and responsibilities, then the rationale behind the decision should be shown. If it is possible to break down the entire project into specific activity elements, it should be done. This will give the prospective client the impression that planning has been done and that care has been taken to analyze the project and to determine how resources can best be managed in order to accomplish the task.

Company Organization

Some clients want information on the organizational structure of the consulting firm that will be performing the work. This information should be contained in the organization and management section of the proposal.

The consultant should include the firm's personnel, equipment, and facilities to assure the prospective client of your firm's capability to support the project. An organization chart of your firm may be included here. If you plan to "farm out" sections of the project to outside experts, you should provide details and inform the prospective client of provisions made to control quality and meet time schedules. There is no need to include pricing arrangements concerning outsourcing.

The client would want to know that adequate measures have been established, or will be established, to control cost. Thus, the cost control system that will be in place should be described in this section of the proposal. This will assure the prospective client that the proposed project will not be hampered by an inadequate cost management system. You should use this section of your proposal to convince the prospective client that your firm places great emphasis on financial responsibility.

Assignment (Project) Organization

It is a good idea to indicate the human resources that will be allocated to the proposed assignment. The identity and capability of the individual who will be responsible for seeing that the work is accomplished as scheduled and within costs should be included in this section of the proposal. It is important to indicate the relationship between the assignment (project) leader and company management. This will serve to assure the prospective client that the project will have the full support of the entire organization.

In this section of the proposal, the consultant should indicate the relationship between the project organization and the client's organization. It is in this section of the proposal that the consultant discusses the arrangements for inter-organizational communication. Questions about who reports to whom and who is responsible for providing certain information are addressed in this section of the proposal. The methods to be used in evaluating and reporting on the progress and status of the assignment should also be stated in this section of the proposal.

Résumés

There is a tendency for consultants to neglect or downplay this aspect of the proposal. This is a mistake that you must avoid. The prospective client is likely to place some weight on the education, training, and experience of the key personnel who will be involved in the assignment. Of course, the résumés should be up to date, and all irrelevant information should be omitted. In presenting the résumés, you should include the following areas:

Education It is often not sufficient just to mention the certificates, diplomas, and degrees of the key personnel. Mention should be made of the level of academic achievement, areas of study, and the topics of any dissertations, theses, or articles published by the key personnel. Books published and certification by a consulting association or institution are always very influential.

Experience Generalized experience in the area of the proposed work is important, but even more important is specialized experience, experience identical to that required to perform the work. Any management experience relevant to the proposed assignment should be included, and specific goal accomplishments and recognition of outstanding performance should be noted.

Company Success

A successful track record in the area of the proposed project is usually included in this section of the proposal if the consulting firm has such a track record. Information about the consulting firm's actual performance on an identical or similar project will be an effective means of convincing the prospective client of your firm's capability to perform the task effectively and efficiently. Complimentary references from past satisfied clients could be used effectively in this section of the proposal.

The Cost Section

Some clients require a detailed breakdown of the cost elements in the proposal, while others require only a fixed fee quotation. The thing to keep in mind is that the proposed fee must appear reasonable to the prospective client, otherwise, the prospective client will not attach much credibility to your cost proposal. One way of establishing credibility is to relate your fee to the material and human resources that will be used on the proposed project and the time that the proposed project will require. Even the most high-priced and reputable independent consultant will experience difficulty if the proposal fee bears no apparent relationship to the time and resources that will be devoted to the proposed project.

Proposed Payment Plan

Many clients base their decisions to use the services of a consultant on the terms of payment. This is particularly the case with individual (as opposed to business) clients. But even some business clients will appreciate a convenient payment plan. The proposed terms of payment should be clearly indicated in this section of the proposal. If the fee quoted includes the cost of follow-up and monitoring activities, then it should be indicated in the cost section of the proposal.

THE FORMAT OF THE PROPOSAL

The proposal should be organized in a convenient manner. The following format is recommended:

1. Letter of Transmittal
2. Front Material
3. Executive Summary
4. Proposal Body
5. Appendices

The Letter of Transmittal

The letter of transmittal is an important document, and, if properly written, can stimulate the prospective client to read the proposal. The opening paragraph of the letter of transmittal should briefly describe the proposed assignment. The letter of transmittal should include references to the request for proposal, if applicable. References should also be made to any telephone conversations and interviews held with the prospective client. You should also use the letter of transmittal to draw the prospective client's attention to any unusual terms or conditions in the proposal.

The letter of transmittal provides an excellent opportunity for the consultant to shout the praises of his/her consulting firm. Use it. If applicable, do not be hesitant to state that your firm has had tremendous success with similar engagements. Indicate that it makes good business sense for the prospective client to engage your services to perform the proposed work.

Front Matter

The front matter includes:

A. Title page
B. Proprietary page
C. Table of contents

The *title page* bears the title of the proposed project; the client's name; the name, address, and telephone number of the consultant; and the date. The *proprietary page* usually states that the proposal should be used only for the purpose for which it was intended, and should not be transmitted to anyone else. In a voluminous proposal, a *table of contents* is a useful guide to the prospective client. It shows the various sections of the proposal, and if the prospective client wishes to find any particular section, the table of contents points him/her to the relevant page. If the proposal contains only a few pages, a table of contents is not necessary.

The Executive Summary

The executive summary is a summary of the entire proposal. In preparing this summary, you should put your best foot forward. The prospective client will often decide based on the prospective summary whether or not he/she is interested in your proposal. A good executive summary will convince the prospective client that it is worthwhile to study and evaluate your proposal for serious consideration. Your executive summary should address the prospective client's problem directly. For obvious reasons, the executive summary is written *after* the proposal has been written.

The proposal Body

As noted earlier, the body of the proposal consists of three main sections: the technical section, the organization and management section, and the cost section. In some instances, each of these sections may constitute a volume in itself, each volume being written by a different writer. In such cases, care must be taken to ensure that there are no conflicts or inconsistencies between the various volumes. The three volumes should be consistent in format, terminology, abbreviations used, and type font. There should be a perceived unity in structure.

It is more likely, however, that the proposal submitted by an independent consultant will be written by himself/herself or by a member of his/her staff. Even in this case, the writer should make sure that there are no contradictions between these three sections of the proposal. The sections must be compatible with each other and with other proposal documents.

Appendices

Additional information that you may want the prospective client to have can be included in appendices. Documents such as financial statements, annual reports, descriptions of facilities, charts, and tables are appropriate for appendices.

COVERS AND BINDINGS

Your proposal is in competition with several others for an assignment that you consider to be important, otherwise, why would you spend valuable time preparing and submitting it for evaluation and consideration? Numerous phrases have been used to emphasize the importance of first impressions. The covers and bindings of your proposal will make either a favorable or unfavorable impression. Let the covers and binders of your proposal score "first impression" points for you.

An interesting and attractive cover and binding will motivate the prospective client to see what's inside. This author always tries to select a display for the cover that is somehow related to the title of the proposal. This makes the proposal presentation more meaningful. Laminated covers are also impressive. It is totally unacceptable to place an unbound proposal in an envelope and send it off to a prospective client. Your proposal will not be judged entirely by its cover, but attractive covers and bindings will score points.

SAMPLES OF PROPOSALS

We have looked at different aspects of proposals. In order to illustrate the various aspects discussed, we shall consider examples of two proposals: a short proposal, and a longer proposal in the appendix at the end of the chapter. Space would not permit us to illustrate a voluminous proposal. Keep in mind also that our examples may not contain every single aspect of proposals. Our aim is to illustrate the most common elements.

Example of a Short Proposal

This type of proposal is often referred to as a Letter Proposal. It is usually written after a meeting with a client who has informally engaged your services.

Dear Mr. Smith:

I thoroughly enjoyed our meeting on September 12, 20___ and our discussions about work to be performed for your company. I appreciate your confidence in our firm, and I assure you that we will do our best to satisfy your needs.

The main purpose of this letter is to formally confirm our mandate for this engagement and to outline the terms of this engagement.

Objectives

The primary objective of this assignment is to provide the Board of Directors and management of ABC Corporation with relevant data and other material necessary to enable the Company to accomplish its immediate and short-term objectives efficiently and effectively.

Specific Services to be Provided

We propose to perform the following functions for ABC Corporation.

1. A detailed fact-finding study and analysis of the financial position of the ABC _____ project, leading to an accurate estimate of the amount of money required to complete the project.

2. *An immediate training needs assessment of the Company's personnel and actual implementation of training* **at all levels** *as the needs assessment exercise may indicate.*

3. *The formulation of specific procedures to guide the actions of the Board and management so that conflicts will be minimized and both direction and management be made more effective.*

4. *The design and production of* **appropriate** *performance appraisal forms for ABC Corporation.*

Reports

We will issue timely and selective interim reports during the execution of this assignment. A comprehensive report on all phases of the assignment will be delivered upon completion of the engagement.

Cost and Timing

The total estimated cost of the completed assignment is $_____, one half ($___) payable on authorization to proceed (i.e., September 12, 20___), invoice attached, and one-half payable on delivery of the final report, two copies of which will be delivered in its final form.

The engagement, including appropriate management and staff training, will be completed no later than December 31, 20__.

Please indicate your agreement with the terms of this engagement by signing below, and returning a copy of the signed page only to us.

Sincerely,

Engagement Agreement

I agree to the terms outlined above and hereby confirm the verbal authorization given on September 12, 20__.

_____

J. Smith
General Manager
ABC Corporation

Note how easily and conveniently the letter proposal has been turned into a contract.

CHAPTER SUMMARY

1. A proposal is a document that outlines a plan of action to be followed in performing an assignment. The proposal details what will be done, but not how it will be done.

2. A consulting proposal should convince the prospective client that the consultant is capable of solving the client's problem.

3. It is necessary to write proposals because clients request them, they assist in securing assignments, competitors write them, they prepare the consultant for the actual work, they provide guidelines for performance, and they are communication devices.

4. The ultimate objective of the proposal is to bring the prospective client to the point where he/she decides to give the writer the assignment.

5. The main parts of a proposal are the technical section, the organization and management section, and the cost section.

6. A proposal may be organized around the following headings: letter of transmittal; front material consisting of title page, proprietary page and table of contents; executive summary; proposal body; and appendix.

7. The proposal cover and binding should impress the prospective client that the consultant takes pride in his/her work, and that the consultant has respect for his/her client.

APPENDIX

A Sample Proposal

A PROPOSAL TO ABC CORPORATION

FOR

- **THE PREPARATION OF COMPANY MANUALS**
- **THE DEVELOPMENT OF A BUSINESS PLAN**
- **A COMPREHENSIVE DIAGNOSTIC ANALYSIS**

Prepared By:

John Smith, C.I.C.
NEW AGE CONSULTING
123 Main Street
Any Town, Any Province
Any Country
Tel. (012) 345 6789

1. BACKGROUND

The ABC Corporation is a relatively new entrant into the _____industry. The company provides a variety of services including _____ and _____ activities. The company plans to be a major player in the traditional _____ and _____ markets, but expects to assume an active role in other areas such as _____ and _____ as well.

Through the expertise that it will develop in the _____ and _____ fields, ABC Corporation plans to be in a position to provide consultative services in those areas where its abilities and experience will be beneficial to its clients.

In order to accomplish its objectives effectively and efficiently, the company is prepared to take appropriate measures. It realizes that it must have a sound organizational structure that is consistent with its operation, and that adequate management and control devices must be put in place in order to facilitate implementation.

The company wants to be in a position where it can easily take advantage of business opportunities as they present themselves, and take corrective or evasive measures to prevent bottlenecks and other threats to its growth and development.

2. PROPOSED SERVICES

The primary objective of this engagement would be to conduct a complete examination of the internal organizational structure and operations of the ABC Corporation, and to make recommendations for the effective and efficient management of the organization. More specifically, the following services would be provided: (list services)

....

....

....

....

....

....

The proposed study will cover the following areas:

- Corporate and departmental plans and objectives
- Organizational structure
- Policies, systems and procedures
- Human resources (personnel) management
- Operations and methods of control
- Internal communication
- Employee morale and perception of the firm

The profitability of your company depends on the degree of efficiency of each of the above areas. In a small firm, even one weak link can spell disaster.

3. APPROACH TO THE PROPOSED ASSIGNMENT

The specific approach that would normally be followed in conducting the proposed assignment is outlined below and illustrated in the following **work-flow diagram**. The first step will be an initial interview with top management to determine the details of the engagement.

- ➤ Project planning
- ➤ Development of appropriate tools
- ➤ Data collection
- ➤ Interviewing
- ➤ Data recording
- ➤ Data analysis and computations
- ➤ General report preparation
- ➤ Writing and production of manuals
- ➤ Writing and production of business plan
- ➤ Monitoring and follow up reports

WORKFLOW DIAGRAM

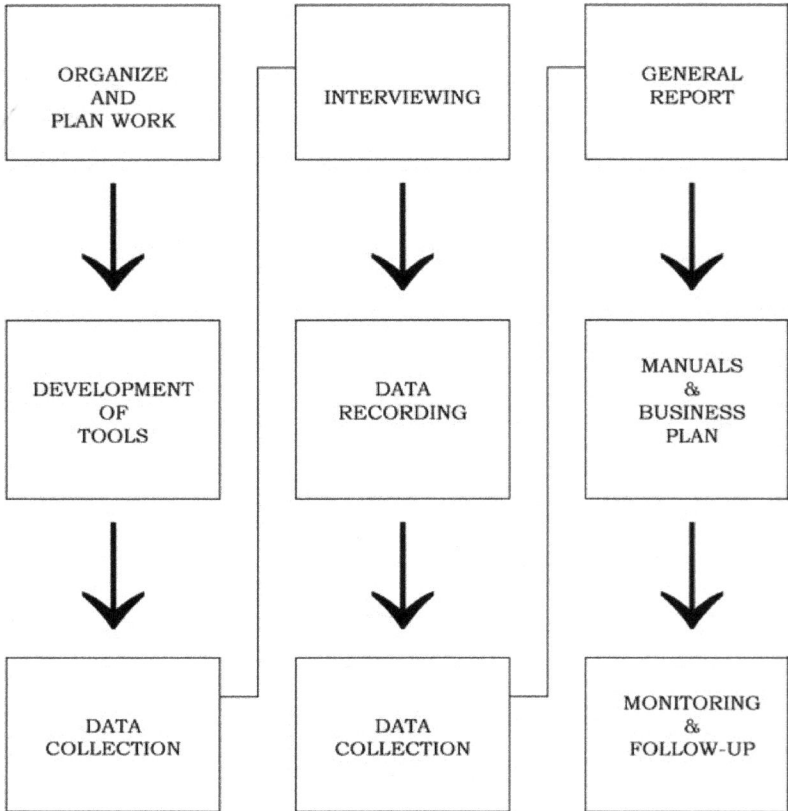

ORGANIZE AND PLAN WORK	INTERVIEWING	GENERAL REPORT
↓	↓	↓
DEVELOPMENT OF TOOLS	DATA RECORDING	MANUALS & BUSINESS PLAN
↓	↓	↓
DATA COLLECTION	DATA COLLECTION	MONITORING & FOLLOW-UP

As is the case with all New Age Consulting assignments, a team approach will be used on this proposed project. Group meetings will allow our consultants to combine their experience in the development of appropriate conclusions and recommendations. In executing this proposed engagement, New Age will employ scientific methods of data collection to gather relevant information. The methods will include the use of questionnaires and interviews. New Age will use appropriate statistical techniques to analyze the data collected.

From the onset, an attempt will be made to establish a favorable relationship between New Age and the management and staff of your company. Both management, staff, and employees will be involved in the diagnostic process. This approach will facilitate the implementation of recommendations and maximize the probability of the success of the entire exercise.

New Age Consulting will present a final General Report that is written in plain English, with recommendations for implementation by management personnel.

4. PROPOSED WORK SCHEDULE

Normal Track

On the normal track, New Age can begin to work on this project as soon as written authorization is received and will have all work completed and delivered to you in approximately 90 days thereafter. The approximate time (in weeks) required for each function is illustrated in the following **Work Schedule** diagram.

WORK SCHEDULE (NORMAL TRACK)

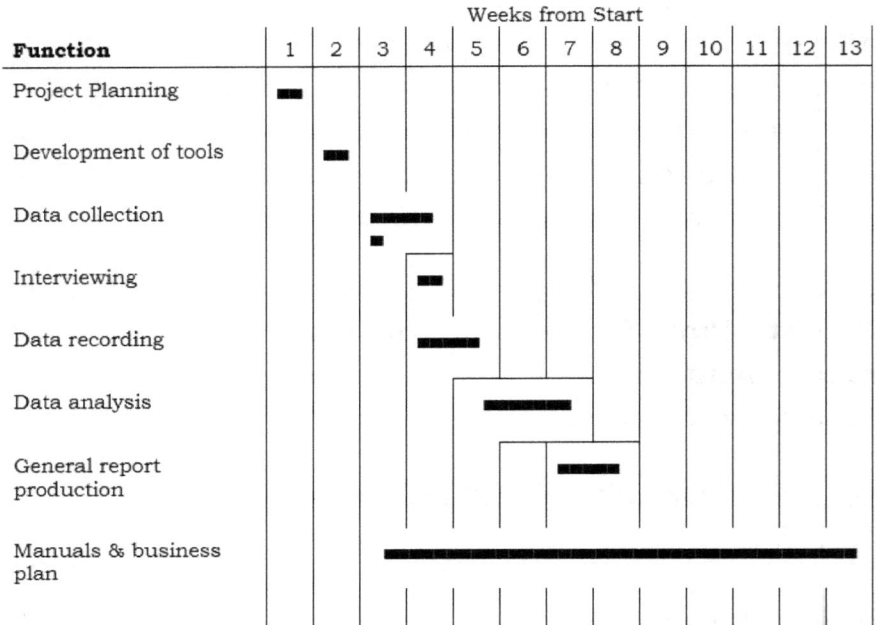

Function	Weeks from Start												
	1	2	3	4	5	6	7	8	9	10	11	12	13
Project Planning	▬												
Development of tools		▬											
Data collection			▬▬▬										
Interviewing				▬▬									
Data recording				▬▬▬									
Data analysis						▬▬▬▬							
General report production							▬▬▬▬						
Manuals & business plan			▬▬▬▬▬▬▬▬▬▬▬▬▬▬▬▬▬▬▬▬▬▬										

Accelerated (Fast) Track

If it is desired to complete the project in a shorter time, an accelerated (fast) track option can be employed. The accelerated approach involves substantially more overlapping of functions and enables the completion of the project in a much shorter time.

Special Circumstances

In view of the special circumstances existing at ABC Corporation, We propose that the assignment begin with the following three activities:

1. The establishment by New Age of proper systems of accounting and record keeping at ABC Corporation

2. The production by New Age of an *interim* Procedures Manual for the accounting and record-keeping system

3. The production of an Organization Manual for ABC Corporation.

The interim Procedures Manual for the accounting and record-keeping system will have the following essential characteristics:

a) The system will ensure that the recording of all transactions is properly executed. This will ensure that no fictitious transactions are perpetrated without detection.

b) The system will institute procedures to ensure that transactions and all relevant commitments are properly and duly authorized.

c) A system to preserve the integrity of all accounting records will be put in place to make sure that all transactions are properly recorded.

d) Checks and balances will be built into the system to prevent errors in billings and recording transactions. Clear procedures on this aspect will be provided.

e) The procedure will ensure that all transactions are properly classified. This will necessitate the designing of a Chart of Accounts that will respond to the company's special needs. It will be tailor-made to facilitate report preparation, to provide an adequate description of each account and a clear distinction of each.

f) Standard Journal Vouchers and other vouchers that may be deemed relevant, based on our assessment, will be designed.

g) Policies and procedures will be put in place with regard to fixed asset purchases and the amortization of assets. Safeguards to protect company assets will be built into the system.

h) The system we envisage will ensure that duties are assigned in such a way that adequate segregation of duties will be attained. This will be designed taking into consideration the size of the accounting personnel.

i) Accounting information becomes relevant only if it is produced on a timely basis. An appropriate computer-based accounting system will be considered, taking into account the special needs of the company together with the expertise of the key personnel.

Note: The proposed final document will also outline the responsibilities and the general interrelationships of the key personnel in the accounting department, and also the role of auditing in the company.

If only the three activities outlined above under **Special Circumstances** are considered, the fee would be $_____ one-half payable on authorization to proceed and one-half payable on delivery of work. The assignment will be completed within the 18-day period stipulated in your request.

Follow Up and Monitoring

In order for your company to maximize its returns from this proposed engagement, a monitoring system has been built into this proposal. It is proposed that the principal consultant work closely with the senior management of your company during the first six months following the delivery of the manuals and business plan.

The consultant will serve as a resource person to guide management during the implementation stages of this project and will provide periodic progress reports. This aspect of the proposed assignment is vital for the success of the project and hence the profitability of your company.

5. NEW AGE QUALIFICATIONS

The Team Leader for this proposed assignment will be John Smith, MBA, C.I.C. Mr. Smith is a distinguished professor of business and management, and a prominent management, business, and economic consultant. Mr. Smith has been the team leader for most of the projects undertaken by New Age. A prolific writer, he has to his credit the publication of several books and articles in the fields of business and management. ***His How to Organize a Successful Business*** has been a top seller since its publication two years ago.

Mr. Smith will be assisted on this proposed project by a

competent staff consisting of: (List staff and their qualifications).

Firm Background

Established in 1985, New Age Consulting has provided services to numerous organizations from a wide variety of industries and governments, both nationally and internationally. Among the clients of New Age are manufacturing establishments, banks, mortgage and trust companies, hospitals, retailers in various industries, educational institutions, and many other organizations. These organizations and businesses received assistance from New Age in virtually every aspect of management and organization.

New Age is eminently qualified to deliver the proposed services and to guide your firm through the formulation of sound business decision-making -- decisions that will ensure the profitability of your business, and secure the financial future of the company.

(Note: The actual names of some of your recent clients could be mentioned here, and complimentary references could be included).

6. SUMMARY OF BENEFITS

- New Age is quite familiar with the internal organizational structures and relationships of successful businesses. By engaging New Age for this assignment, your company will gain the benefit of our extensive experience in management and organization, thereby assuring that the proposed services will be delivered satisfactorily.

- New Age has expertise in business problem-solving. Unlike many other consulting firms, New Age does not "farm out" work to outside or freelance consultants. Instead, all our work is done in-house. ABC Corporation will gain the benefit of the high quality of service that accompanies constant quality control.

- The New Age consultants slated for this assignment possess a balance of organizational, technical, and communication backgrounds, thereby providing the disciplines necessary for efficient delivery of the proposed services.

- The entire organization mission of New Age is dedicated to the business of assisting clients in improving the effectiveness of their managerial decision-making so that their profit and other business objectives can be realized. Therefore, this effort is not secondary or incidental to other New Age services. It is the central focus of its organizational experience and expertise.

7. COST OF PROPOSED SERVICES

Fees are established on the basis of the number of person-hours that will be spent on the project at standard rates for various levels of consulting staff. Accordingly, our fees for the entire project will be $_____.

Note 1: These fees include all expenses and follow-up and monitoring activities as outlined above in Section 4.

Note 2: The standard policy of New Age is to charge a fixed fee of $_____ for solicited proposals such as this. If New Age is offered an engagement resulting from the proposal, then there is no charge for the proposal.

PROPOSED PAYMENT PLAN

In order not to compromise the cash flow position of ABC Corporation, we suggest that payment be made in installments as indicated in the following Payment Schedule.

Scheduled Payment Date   Amount

1st payment Upon authorization to proceed $_____
2nd payment One month after authorization   _____
3rd payment On completion and delivery of report

_____

We propose a payment of $____ per month during the monitoring and follow-up period.

We trust that you will find this proposal acceptable and we look forward to working with you on this most important project.

If you have any questions or suggestions pertaining to this proposal or any other assignment you would like accomplished, please do not hesitate to contact us.

If the terms of this proposal are acceptable to you, please sign below the authorization for New Age to proceed and return the original to us.

Sincerely yours,

_____

Authorization to Proceed

_____

I agree to the terms in the above proposal and grant authorization to proceed in accordance with these terms.

_____ Date_____

Signature

SELF-TEST QUESTIONS

Indicate whether each of the following is true (T) or false (F).

1. _____ Except for communication consultants, writing skills are not particularly important to a consultant. What is important is the ability to solve the client's problem.

2. _____ A mistake that is often made among independent consultants is to consider a proposal a sales document.

3. _____ The main objective of a proposal is to influence the prospective client to use your consulting services.

4. _____ A proposal should detail *how* the consultant intends to perform an assignment and not just *what* he/she intends to do.

5. _____ The desire for clients to know what quality of service they can expect for their money is an important reason for writing proposals.

6. _____ It is never necessary to submit written proposals in order to obtain engagements.

7. _____ An independent consultant should never submit a written proposal unless it is specifically requested by a prospective client.

8. _____ The preparation of a proposal may cause the actual work to flow more smoothly just by virtue of having prepared a proposal.

9. _____ If a consultant knows what he/she is about, it will not be necessary to refer to the proposal during the performance of the assignment.

10. _____ Proposals are of value only to the prospective clients. This explains why consultants are so reluctant to prepare and submit them.

11. _____ Whereas sales letters should exemplify the AIDA approach, this condition or requirement is not necessary in the case of proposals.

12. _____ The quality of a proposal serves as an indication of the quality of work that the client can expect from the consultant who writes the proposal.

13. _____ The organization and management section is the most important part of a proposal.

14. _____ The technical section of a proposal should outline the work to be performed, the methodology that will be used, and the time for the completion of each phase.

15. _____ Diagrams, schedules and charts are two technical and should therefore not be included in proposals.

16. _____ Complicated diagrams that are difficult to understand may do more harm than good in a proposal, as they may detract from the

information that the proposer is trying to provide.

17. _____ A description of the means of accomplishing the proposed task should not be included in the proposal.

18. _____ In establishing the time required to complete an assignment, the consultant should ignore overlapping activities.

19. _____ To be on the safe side, a consultant should never indicate in a proposal the time allotted to the completion of each phase of the project.

20. _____ If possible, an entire consulting engagement (project) should be broken down into specific activity elements.

21. _____ An independent consultant should never let a prospective client know that he/she plans to "farm out" sections of an engagement to outside experts.

22. _____ A consulting proposal is not an application for employment. Therefore it should not include resumés of the consultants who will work on the project.

23. _____ One way of establishing the credibility of your cost proposal is to relate your fee to the material and human resources that will be used on the proposed project and the time that the proposed project will require.

24. _____ One of the objectives of the executive summary of a proposal is to convince the prospective client that it is worth while to study and evaluate your proposal.

25. _____ If a prospective client requests a proposal, the consultant need not be concerned about the cover and binding of the proposal because the prospective client is already interested and curious about the content of the proposal.

26. _____ If timing is a crucial factor, it is quite acceptable to place an unbound proposal in an envelope and send it off to a prospective client.

27. _____ A letter proposal and a contract are completely different documents and no attempt should be made to combine them.

ANSWERS

1. F   2. F   3. T   4. F   5. T   6. F   7. F   8. T

9. F   10. F   11. F   12. T   13. F   14. T   15. F   16. T

17. F   18. F   19. F   20. T   21. F   22. F   23. T   24. T

25. F   26. F   27. F

CHAPTER 8
REPORT WRITING

INTRODUCTION

Most consulting engagements culminate in a written report with recommendations to be implemented so that the client's problem can be solved. It is via reports that you communicate with your clients. This does not mean that some form of verbal report may not be given, but a formal written report is generally considered to be in order.

In this chapter, our attention will be focused on an important aspect of independent consulting: report writing. Many of the considerations we discussed in the previous chapter dealing with proposal writing apply also to report writing. Under report writing, our main concern will be with formal reports. We will study the parts of a report and pay some attention to report presentation.

Let's assume that you submitted a winning proposal. The prospective client has chosen your consulting firm to do the work. You and your team have done an excellent job in dealing with the assignment. Now, you must prepare a written report for your client. The information that you present to your client must be written so that it is easy to read and understand. Good report writing can secure further engagements for you. Indeed, many future assignments have been won or lost on the basis of good or poor report writing. A poorly presented report suggests that you have little or no respect for your client, and shows that you do not really take pride in your work. The purpose of this chapter is to help the independent consultant to write and present good reports.

DEFINITION OF REPORT

There are numerous types of reports, but our interest in this chapter concerns reports written by independent consultants for their clients. A report, regardless of its type, may be defined as *an account of some activity that is transmitted to someone for a specific purpose*. A report conveys specific information to a specific reader or to specific readers. In our context, the report is usually an answer to a question or a response to a request for particular information.

REASONS FOR WRITING REPORTS

Probably the most obvious reason for writing a report is that the client who engages your services expects a written account of the work that you have done. But there are other reasons for writing reports. The report that you write for a business client may be considered as a record of work performed. Moreover, many of the reports that consultants write form the basis for important business and organizational decisions. A written report allows the client to study its contents and serves as a handy reference from time to time.

THE STRUCTURE (FORMAT) OF THE REPORT

There is really no *standard* format for a consulting report. Different consultants tend to use different structures. The most appropriate format will depend on current practices in the field, the purpose of the report, and the length of the report. A key factor to keep in mind is that the report should be structured to fit the account that you want to give. However, it is safe to say that the final report should contain the following general topics:

> Introduction
>
> Report Body
>
> Conclusion
>
> Recommendations.

The following is the general structure that we recommend.

- Title page
- Table of contents
- Preface or Foreword
- Terms of Reference
- Executive summary
- Introduction
- Purpose

- Procedure
- Analysis
- Comments and Recommendations
- Appendices

Title Page

The title page should contain the following information:

- Title of the report
- Name of the client
- Name(s) of the consultant(s) and firm
- Date

Report Title

The title of the report should indicate briefly the main activity on which the consultant is reporting. For example, if the consultant was asked to analyze operations at the ABC Corporation with the objective of increasing efficiency, the title of the report could be:

AN ANALYSIS OF OPERATIONS AT ABC CORPORATION

The entire title may be capitalized, or only the first letter of each word (except articles, propositions, and conjunctions) may be capitalized. The following style is thus acceptable:

An Analysis of Operations at ABC Corporation

Name of the Client

The name of the client is usually preceded by the phrase: *Prepared for* or *Submitted to*. The name of the client is usually capitalized as shown in the following sample:

Prepared for:

ABC CORPORATION

Name of the Consultant and Firm

The client for whom the report is written will, in all likelihood, receive many other reports as time progresses. The name of the consultant and the firm on the report serve to identify you and your firm as the consultant who did the work.

From a marketing point of view, it is important to have the name of your firm on the title page. Your report will likely be read by many people, so it could actually help to "sell" your consulting services.

The name of the consultant/firm is generally preceded by the phrase: *Prepared by*. The font used for this section of the title page is typically smaller than the fonts used for the title and the name of the client. A sample follows:

Prepared by:
John Smith
New Age Consulting
123 Main Street
Any Town, Any Province
Any Country

Date

The date on which the report was completed appears on the title page. Remember the correct style for writing dates.

Correct: October 17, 20 or 17th October, 20___
Incorrect: October 17th, 20___

Report Number

Some consultants number their reports for convenience. If you use a report number, it should appear on the title page. Report numbers are often written as codes. For example, the report for the second assignment completed for the ABC Corporation in June 1998 could be numbered as 9806ABC 02.

Note: The title page is not numbered.

A sample of a title page is shown on the following page.

Illustration 8.1. Sample Title Page

AN ANALYSIS OF OPERATIONS

AT ABC CORPORATION

Prepared for:

ABC CORPORATION

Prepared by:

John Smith, C.I.C.
New Age Consulting
123 Main Street
Any Town, Any Province
Any Country
Tel. (012) 345 6789

Report No. 9806ABC 02

June 25, 1998

Table of Contents

A short report does not really require a table of contents. In a longer report, however, a table of contents helps the reader find material quickly. The following is a sample of a table of contents.

Illustration 8.2. Sample of Table of Contents

TABLE OF CONTENTS

Note that the table of contents includes subheadings with their appropriate page numbers.

Preface

The preface provides a kind of general background to the report. It is good courtesy to acknowledge the assistance and cooperation of people who have helped in the preparation of the report or during the performance of the assignment. Acknowledgements may be made at the end of the preface or they may be made on a separate "acknowledgement page." The following is a sample preface.

Illustration 8.3. Sample Preface

The present report is based on a study conducted at the ABC Corporation by New Age Consulting. The study was authorized by the General Manager under the direction of the Board of Directors of the Corporation, and covered the following broad areas:

- *plans and objectives*
- *organizational structure*
- *operations and methods of control*

Business decision making should ideally be based on solid data. The information provided in this report will be of utmost importance to management in terms of policy formulation and direction.

A project of this magnitude cannot be the effort of any one individual. Many people have contributed in a variety of ways to the completion of the assignment. First, we would like to offer our sincere gratitude to the Board of Directors and the General Manager of ABC Corporation for the confidence they have shown in New Age Consulting by giving us the opportunity to be a part of such an exciting project.

Second, we must say a BIG "Thank You" to the entire staff of ABC Corporation for their willing cooperation and participation in this project. Mr. Brown and Ms. Greene deserve special thanks for their unflinching support even when we dared to encroach on their busy schedules..........

John Smith, C.I.C. (Chief Consultant)
David Joseph, C.C. (Consultant)
Jackie Simpson, C.I.C. (Project Coordinator)

Terms of Reference

The terms of reference spell out the consultant's mandate for the assignment. It usually includes a synopsis of the circumstances that led to the assignment, and it details the specific task that was given to the consultant. Anyone who reads the report should be able to recognize the justification for the assignment. Once the background information has been given, the mandate can be stated as follows:

It was against this background that the services of New Age Consulting were engaged. Details of the specific mandate that was given to New Age Consulting are enumerated below:

Details of the mandate are then stated.

Executive Summary

Your client might want to have a general idea of the contents of your report without having to read the details contained in the entire report. Of course, the client would have to read the report for the details. The executive summary should highlight, in a concise manner, the main points of the report. Depending on the report, the executive summary may be a single paragraph, or it may contain several pages. As a general rule, however, the executive summary should be about one-tenth of the length of the report. It is a matter of good organization to present the material in the executive summary in the same order as presented in the actual report. The executive summary is written *after* the report has been written.

Introduction

The introduction does exactly what its name suggests it introduces your client to the material that is to be found in the report. The introduction sets the stage for the assignment that is being reported on. The introduction provides a background against which the report must be understood. The following is a sample of an introduction:

Illustration 8.4. Sample of Introduction

INTRODUCTION

It is always an exciting experience to be involved in a new project, and especially so when the venture shows great potential for success. The ABC Corporation is in a position to contribute significantly to the economic development of _____ (region).

When New Age Consulting accepted this assignment, its consultants knew immediately that maximum staff involvement was a major prerequisite for the success of this assignment. We were well aware of the danger of being seen as "outsiders" coming in to "shake up" the organization. We knew that if we did not take certain precautions, there could be resentment from the staff, and this could really hamper our efforts to help the organization to attain its objectives. In order to do our job well, we needed accurate information from the employees.

We knew that the best way to obtain the information that we needed was to have the full support of both management and staff. Accordingly, we wanted the employees to know what we were doing and why we were doing it. We wanted them to know that their input was important. It was important for our consultants to know as much as possible about ABC Corporation and its operation, and we felt that the employees were a good source of information.

A great deal of information about the structure and operation of any organization can be obtained by carefully analyzing the following three interest areas upon which the study would focus:

- *Plans and objectives*
- *Organizational structure*
- *Operations and methods of control.*

Each of the above areas was carefully studied in order to determine the organization's strengths and weaknesses and to assess what needed to be done to move the organization forward.

Purpose

The purpose of the assignment usually follows the introduction. In some reports, the purpose is presented as a sub-section of the introduction. The purpose includes:

- A statement of the legitimacy of the assignment (who requested the study)
- A statement of why the assignment was requested
- A statement of what the assignment intended to accomplish

The legitimacy of the assignment could be stated as follows:

> *The study was requested by the General Manager and Chief Executive Officer (CEO) of ABC Corporation, under the direction and authority of the Board of Directors of the Corporation.*

The reason for requesting the assignment could be stated as follows:

> *The main objectives of the study were to provide management with the most accurate and analytical view of operations at ABC Corporation, to investigate the Corporation's strengths and weaknesses and to draw these to the attention of management, to indicate current and future opportunities that may be exploited, and to make recommendations that will help the organization to achieve its objectives in an effective and efficient manner.*

The intended accomplishments may be stated as follows:

> *The findings of this study will guide management in its decisions in terms of strategic planning in general, and particularly in terms of the three areas of interest listed above. The study will indicate both the strengths and weaknesses of the*

organization and point out specific actions that must be taken in order to correct any deficiencies and thus establish the Corporation firmly on the path to organizational efficiency.

Procedure

The procedure section includes the various steps followed in executing the assignment. Visits to the Company, interviews between the consultant(s) and the client, meetings with staff members, methods of data collection, etc. are all reported in the procedure section of the report.

Analysis

This section forms a significant section of the report. The information collected is presented in a variety of forms such as tables, charts, figures, etc. The analysis should be presented in an orderly manner. For example, plans and objectives could be analyzed first, followed by an analysis of the organizational structure of the Corporation, then an analysis of the operations and methods of control. Remember that in this section, you are reporting exactly what is revealed by your analysis. This is not the place to express your *personal opinions*. You are simply stating the *facts*.

Comments and Recommendations

Comments

If there are many issues on which the consultant wishes to comment or which the consultant wants to discuss, and if there are many recommendations to be made, separate sections may be used for comments and recommendations. The comments/discussion section allows the consultant to interject into the report his/her own subjective interpretation of the results of the analysis. Your client wants to know your expert and professional opinion and it is in this section that you should give it. Your views, of course, are based on or derived from the data that you have analyzed.

Recommendations

The whole purpose of the assignment is to find a solution to the client's problem. On the basis of your analysis, you recommend actions to be taken by your client to solve the problem. It is a good idea to number the recommendations and to list them in the order in which they emerge from the analysis. This author recommends that a rationale be given for each recommendation made. It evokes credibility and thus tends to carry more weight. Take a look at the recommendations to the ABC Corporation contained in Illustration 8.5.

Illustration 8.5. Sample Recommendations

In the area of Plans and Objectives, we recommend:

R1. *That managers constantly explain their department's plans and objectives to their staff, and emphasize each employee's role in the accomplishment of those objectives. Management's expectations should be clearly stated.*

Purpose: *To familiarize employees with corporate plans and objectives so that they can be more effective.*

R2. *That managers/supervisors hold short*

meetings at least once a month with their staff to discuss issues such as the division of responsibilities, punctuality, and task accomplishment as they relate to their particular departments. A variety of problems for which solutions must be found can also be discussed at these meetings.

__Purpose:__ There is some evidence that some employees feel left out of the process. The purpose of this recommendation is to keep the staff informed about happenings in the organization and to obtain their input.

If the consultant recognizes areas for further study, he/she should identify them and add them to the list of recommendations.

Note: It is unethical to suggest areas for further study if the only objective is to provide work for the consultant.

Appendix or Appendices

The appendix provides a convenient means of presenting detailed information which, if included in the main report, may interrupt the smooth flow of the presentation. Only relevant items that would be of interest to the client should be included in the appendix. Appendices may contain the following materials:

- Sample(s) of questionnaire(s) used
- Letters (Be sure to respect confidentiality)
- Tables
- Charts
- Illustrations

If more than one appendix is used, they should be titled so that they are differentiated. For example, they could be titled as: Appendix A, Appendix B, Appendix C, and so on.

CHAPTER SUMMARY

1. A report is an account of some activity that is transmitted to someone for a specific purpose.

2. A report may be verbal or written. Independent consultants often submit written (as opposed to verbal) reports of their assignments.

3. Consultants write reports mainly to convey information to their clients. Reports serve as records of work performed, they form the basis for organizational decision-making and they serve as convenient references.

4. A report may be structured in the following order: title page, table of contents, preface/foreword, terms of reference, executive summary, introduction, purpose, procedure, analysis, comments and recommendations, and appendix.

5. It is a good idea to provide a rationale for each recommendation that is made. It enhances credibility and gives the recommendations a better chance of being implemented.

SELF-TEST QUESTIONS

Indicate whether each of the following is true (T) or false (F).

1. _____ The sole purpose of a report is to give your client a written report of work that you have done.

2. _____ The title page of a report should contain only the title of the report and the date.

3. _____ It is important for the consultant's name to appear on the title page of the report because it may help to market the consultant's services.

4. _____ A table of contents may be included in a proposal but never in a report.

5. _____ It is appropriate to include acknowledgements at the end of the preface.

6. _____ The client already knows the terms of reference for an engagement. It is therefore unnecessary to include terms of reference in the report.

7. _____ The analysis section of the report offers a splendid opportunity for the consultant to express his/her personal and professional opinion on the project.

8. _____ A "Comments" section of a report allows the consultant to convey his/her expert opinion to the client.

9. _____ Giving the rationale for each recommendation made in a report makes the recommendation more credible.

10. _____ An independent consultant should never recommend any further studies to a client, because the client will think that the consultant is simply making work for himself/herself.

11. _____ The success of a consulting practice depends, to a great extent, on the consultant's ability to write good reports.

12. _____ The consultant should submit a final report upon completion of an assignment, but he/she should avoid submitting interim reports at all costs.

13. _____ There is a standard format for report writing among independent consultants, and it is the responsibility of all independent consultants to be familiar with that standard.

14. _____ A consultant may use a report number for his/her own convenience, but such a number should not appear anywhere in the report to the client.

15. _____ In the preface, the consultant provides a general background to the report.

16. _____ The purpose of a proposed assignment should be included in the proposal but it should not appear in the report.

17. _____ An appendix serves no useful purpose because any material placed in an appendix can be conveniently included in the main body of the report.

18. _____ The title page is the appropriate place to indicate the name of the client for whom the report is prepared.

ANSWERS

1. F   2. F   3. T   4. F   5. T   6. F   7. F   8. T

9. T   10. F   11. T   12. F   13. F   14. F   15. T   16. F

17. F   18. T

CHAPTER 9
THE INTERVIEW

INTRODUCTION

Engagements are won largely by your proposals and the initial interview. In Chapter 7, we studied proposal writing in some detail. We will devote this entire chapter to a discussion of the initial interview with your potential client. In most cases, the independent consultant will be invited to meet with the prospective client. This interview should be taken very seriously. Even though you are not applying for a job as an employee, you may be competing with other consultants for the assignment. There are appropriate and inappropriate dress and behavior as far as the interview is concerned. You may blow the whole deal if you don't know how to dress and how to act.

We begin the chapter with a discussion of the decision to attend an interview. We then examine appropriate appearance and behavior at an interview and offer a list of rating factors used by interviewers. Next, we turn our attention to the purpose of the interview, indicating the information you should obtain at the interview. We then present a list of mistakes that are sometimes made at the interview, after which, we indicate typical questions asked at interviews. We end the chapter with a discussion of effective interviewing.

SHOULD YOU ATTEND AN INTERVIEW?

For a variety of reasons, people don't accept all invitations. The same is true of invitations by prospective clients for consultants to attend interviews. It is, in this author's opinion, pointless to attend an interview if you suspect that the prospective client has no intention of engaging your services. In deciding whether or not to attend an interview, you could make use of the concept of *expected value*. Let's assume that you will earn $20,000.00 from an assignment and that the probability (likelihood) of your getting the assignment is 0.50 (that is, you have a 50/50 chance of getting the assignment). In that case, the expected value of the assignment is 50% of $20,000.00 = $10,000. If the probability of receiving the assignment were only 5%, then the expected value would be only 5% of $20,000.00 = $1,000.00. If the total cost of attending the interview (travel time, travel cost, preparation time, etc.) exceeds $1,000.00, then from a purely economic point of view, it would not be worth your while to attend that interview.

As can be deduced from the foregoing example, the amount of the contract, the probability of obtaining the assignment, and the cost of attending the interview are important factors in deciding whether or not you will attend an interview. In figuring out the cost of attending an interview, it is important not to ignore the *opportunity cost.* Opportunity cost is a term that economists use for the idea of the alternative that is sacrificed when a choice is made. If you are not currently engaged on an assignment, and you are invited to an interview, the opportunity cost of attending the interview is practically zero. If however, you have to leave off working on an assignment in order to attend the interview, then the opportunity cost is the income you could have earned working on the assignment. Income foregone must be included in your calculation of the cost of attending an interview.

APPEARANCE AND BEHAVIOUR

If you decide that you ought to attend an interview, then your behavior and your appearance should convey an air of professionalism. The first impression you make on your prospective client may determine whether you get an opportunity to sell yourself and your firm, or whether the interview experiences a premature termination. The image that you project at this initial interview should be positive and should speak volumes on your behalf. The importance of your appearance and your behavior cannot be exaggerated.

Let's turn our attention to dress. The way you dress indeed goes a long way in making that first impression. Appropriate dress will help in your effort to make the most favorable impression possible on your prospective client because an attractive personal appearance tends to impress clients favorably. Moreover, the fact that you are well-groomed and appropriately dressed will make you feel comfortable and confident — two qualities that will work for you during the interview. To the extent that it is possible and practical, it is best to dress and groom in ways similar to your prospective client.

Your personal appearance is not the only factor upon which you will be evaluated. Although you are not being interviewed as an employee, your potential clients will tend to use the same rating factors used to evaluate their regular employees. The following is a list of common rating factors:

- personal appearance
- alertness
- speech
- personality
- manners

By studying the above rating factors, you will learn what is in the mind of the potential client during the interview.

I have conducted several interviews, and if an interviewee arrives late, he/she starts with a negative value on my evaluation card. There is hardly any justification for not being on time for an interview. It's a good idea to arrive at the place of an interview about ten minutes early. These few minutes can be used to reduce anxiety and to maintain your composure. If there is any delay beyond your control, you should immediately telephone the prospective client and briefly explain the reason for the delay that places you off schedule.

Upon your arrival at the interview venue, introduce yourself politely to the receptionist or secretary, and offer your card. Give your name clearly and say that you have an appointment with Mr.... at 10:00 a.m. If you are invited to wait, do so patiently. Remain alert and composed. When the secretary or receptionist indicates that you may go in for the interview, greet your prospective client with a greeting such as, "How do you do, Mr.....?" Do not sit down until your prospective client invites you to do so. During the interview, speak as clearly and as naturally as possible, and look directly at your prospective client during conversation.

Your proposal will contain references to your qualifications and your firm's capability. But the best-written proposal will not provide details of your personality. Your prospective client wants to know whether you are a consultant with whom he/she can work. He/she will normally try to avoid personality clashes.

THE PURPOSE OF THE INTERVIEW

The initial interview serves at least four important purposes. First, it gives the prospective client the opportunity to meet with you face to face, to judge whether or not you are the type of consultant that he/she wishes to engage and to explain the details of the assignment. Second, it gives you, the consultant, the opportunity to verify that you truly understand what you are required to do. Third, this meeting with the prospective client will help to determine whether you really want to accept that assignment. Fourth, it gives you the opportunity to collect pertinent information regarding the assignment.

Information You Should Obtain At the Interview

You should try to obtain the following information before leaving the interview:

1. ***What exactly is the problem*** Before you attend the interview, you will usually have a general idea of the reason for the interview. However, a general idea is not enough to enable you to accept an assignment with confidence. You need to know *exactly* why the prospective client is seeing you. This may require some degree of tact on your part. Do not be overly aggressive but try as much as possible to coax the information out of the prospective client.

2. ***What precisely is your role*** Once you have been considered for, or given an assignment, the prospective client has certain specific expectations. If the problem is identified as lagging sales, you may be expected to increase sales by a specific amount or percentage. Perhaps you are expected to perform a comprehensive organizational diagnosis to identify problems or weaknesses in the organizational structure. Perhaps you are expected to introduce a new performance management system. You must know precisely what the prospective client expects from you. You must leave the interview knowing your role.

3. ***How will your performance be measured*** If the assignment involves a comprehensive organizational diagnostic analysis, then you know you have met your client's expectations when you

complete the diagnosis and submit a written report. If the client expects you to prepare an organization manual, you know that you have done the job when you deliver the final product. On the other hand, if profits are low and the client expects you to increase the profit margin, it is not clear that any increase in profits will meet the client's expectations. Similarly, if labor productivity has been declining and the client expects you to improve productivity, it may not be clear that any improvement will satisfy the client's expectations. In these latter instances, expectations must be stated in concrete numerical terms. For example, the profit expectation could be expressed as a 10 percent increase in profits, while the productivity expectation could be stated as a 15 percent increase in productivity. Of course, a measure of productivity would also have to be agreed upon.

4. **Your main contact** It may be necessary for you to interact with several people during the performance of the assignment, but there will usually be one person who will be considered your main contact. That will usually be the person with whom you will communicate most. It will be the person to whom you will turn for information about the assignment. Make sure you know who is this main contact person. If possible, try to arrange to meet with him or her if it is someone other than the interviewer. It is important for you to know the name, position, telephone number, and e-mail address of the main contact person. It

is a good idea to obtain his/her business card. Also, find out who will be the alternate contact person and obtain the same information about him or her.

A FEW DON'TS

Don't Consult During the Interview

From the prospective client's point of view, the purpose of the interview might well be to get as much free advice as possible. From the perspective of the independent consultant, however, the purpose of an interview is never to give free consulting advice. If the prospective client's problem is so transparent that you can solve it at an initial interview, what reason would the client have for engaging your services? As a matter of fact, even if the problem *appears* to be relatively simple, there may be more to it than meets the eye. You should always take the time to study the problem carefully and to become acquainted with the situation before you attempt to offer any advice. And you should give advice only *after* you have been hired to do so.

As an independent consultant, your most valuable asset is your expertise. You have specialized knowledge and know-how for which clients are willing to pay dearly. It may be true that the best things in life are free, but they include things like air, sunlight, and (some would add) the grace of God. Independent consulting services are not included in that list of "free" things.

Many of my colleagues have related stories of clients who invite them to lunch or dinner after an interview. Sometimes, even before the meal is served, the prospective clients manage to receive several hundred dollars of consulting services for free. By the end of the meal, the prospective clients had virtually all the answers to their problems. The prospective clients never became clients.

I have been fortunate to have been spared that particular experience. Even when I was new to the consulting business, I had always believed in the idea that "independent consultants are paid for their services." It is a philosophy that is near and dear to my heart. Of course, prospective clients do try to get free advice. I simply inform them that I always want to find the best possible solution to my clients' problems; that in order to do so, I must gather the necessary data and analyze them carefully; and that I am sure they (the clients) would not expect any less from me. I deliver this information in a most professional manner, and it has successfully discouraged further attempts on the part of my clients to receive free advice. I believe that it has caused me to receive many assignments.

Don't Allow Yourself to Be Treated Like a Potential Employee

Many potential clients will attempt to treat you like a potential or prospective employee. Remember who you are -- an independent consultant. The consulting relationship is a two-way relationship between consultant and client. Even though you want the assignment, you have something that the potential client wants, otherwise he or she would not be meeting with you. The client has a problem that he or she wants you to solve.

The prospective client may attempt to treat you like a potential employee by asking you to submit a resumé. Many independent consultants willingly accede to this request. My policy is one of non-compliance to such a request. Whenever I am asked to supply a resumé, I politely state that my qualifications and my firm's capabilities are included in the written proposal and that my prospective clients are free to contact any of my clients for references. The effect of this response is to remove any doubts about my credibility and my reputation.

Don't Be Conned into Believing That the Client Has No Money

Many clients will try to convince you that they want to hire you but they do not have money. In fact, many of them have an idea of the cost of engaging a consultant, and if they did not have money, why would they even be talking to you? What they are really trying to do is to get you to reduce your fees. Don't fall for it. If you have established your fees honestly on the basis of what you are worth, then you have no reason to reduce those fees. If the prospective client cannot really afford to pay a fee of $5,000.00, you could suggest a convenient payment plan, or you could suggest that the assignment be broken down into phases and the work is spread over a longer period, if possible. If a suitable arrangement cannot be reached, simple inform the prospective client that you would be willing to consider the assignment when funds become available. This will send a message that your fees are most reasonable and therefore not negotiable.

Don't Accept an Assignment That You Know You Cannot Finish on Time

Understandably, clients want assignments to be completed as quickly as possible, and often, during an interview, they try to get consultants to commit themselves to unreasonably short completion times. Although you will do your best to complete the assignment on time, you should not accept a suggestion to complete a six-month assignment in just three months. Simply draw your prospective client's attention to the time schedule outlined in your proposal, and advise him or her that you will need the time to do the job properly. If you stated in your proposal that the assignment will require approximately 20 people-hours at a total cost of $4,500.00, why would you then, at an interview, accept to complete the assignment in 10 people-hours at the same cost? If you cannot complete an assignment within the time required by the prospective client, state your case and then decline, politely and professionally. I know of cases where clients claimed to have been in a hurry with projects, yet months have passed without awarding the assignments to any consultant.

Don't Quote a Fee on The Spot

It is possible that you may be invited to an interview before you submit a proposal. In this situation, the prospective client may describe the assignment and then ask you to quote a fee. It is not a good idea to quote a fee on the spot. It is often impossible to determine the complexity of a problem unless you study the situation. What appears to be quite simple could turn out to be quite involved. Adopt a professional attitude. Let the prospective client know that you are sensitive to the fact that he or she is in a rush with the project, but that you will need time to study the assignment. Assure him or her that as soon as you get back to your office, you will work out the cost details and fax them to him or her. Many new consultants fall into the trap of quoting fees on the spot, only to find out, much to their chagrin, that their quotation was much too low for the amount of work involved.

Don't Rely on Your Memory

During an interview, many aspects of the assignment will be discussed and many details may be given. You should not rely on your memory to recall everything that transpired. Do take notes. A notebook is probably best for this purpose. There are many occasions where consultants take notes on pieces of paper, only to find that one or more of these bits of paper have been misplaced. Just before the interview begins, take out your notebook and be ready to take notes. During the interview, if you do not understand a point that is being made, do not hesitate to ask the client to repeat it. Also, ask the client to spell names about whose spelling you may not be sure.

I know a few consultants who find it easier to use a tape recorder. I do not recommend using a tape recorder at an interview because I have found it to be somewhat intimidating to the prospective client. The prospective client tends to be more selective when he or she knows that the interview is being recorded, thus you (the consultant) do not get as much information as you would with your notebook.

Don't Prolong the Interview

When the prospective client indicates that the interview is over verbally or by body language, please don't attempt to prolong it further. He or she may use a phrase such as, "Well, Mr. X, it was good that I had this opportunity to discuss the project with you," or he or she may get up and look at his or her watch. In any event, you will sense that the interview has ended. You should thank the prospective client and leave graciously.

WHAT YOU SHOULD ASK FOR

Quite often, the interview follows the submission of a proposal, and the prospective client could decide to engage your services on the spot. Depending on the nature of the assignment, you may have to spend a great deal of time at the client's place of work to gather information. This initial interview will not serve that purpose. However, you can ask for certain items to enable you to begin working on the project. A handy way of knowing what items to ask for at this time is to use a Data Form such as the one shown in illustration 9.1 below.

Illustration 9.1. Data Form

Assignment _____

Company: _____

Address: _____

City: _____

State/Province: _____ Country:_____

Company Officers and Other Key Executives:

_____ _____ _____

_____ _____ _____

_____ _____ _____

_____ _____ _____

Board Members:

_____ _____ _____

_____ _____ _____

_____ _____ _____

Main Contact for this Assignment: _____

Title/Position: _____

Address: _____

City, State/Province, Postal Code: _____

Telephone:_____ e-mail_____

Alternate Contact: _____

Title/Position: _____

Address: _____

City, State/Province, Postal Code:_____

Telephone:_____ e-mail_____

Main Business: _____

Number of Employees: _____

Note: Please obtain:

1. Relevant organization charts

2. Financial statements

3. Annual report.

TYPICAL QUESTIONS ASKED AT INTERVIEWS

It would be helpful for you to be acquainted with some typical questions that prospective clients ask during interviews. Knowing these questions will help you prepare for the interview. Of course, there is no guarantee that any of these questions will be asked at *your* interview. Nevertheless, the feeling of preparedness will give you a sense of confidence. Even though many of the answers may be contained in your proposal, the prospective client may ask them nonetheless. We will use a "☼" to alert you of traps that you should avoid. Recall our discussion about a few don'ts earlier in this chapter.

1. What qualifications do you have that make you feel you will succeed in this assignment?

2. What experience have you had with this kind of work?

3. Have you done any assignments that are similar to this one?

4. If you are awarded this contract, who else will be working with you?

5. What prompted you to submit a proposal?

6. What other kind of consulting do you do?

7. We do not seem to have your curriculum vitae on file, will you rush it to us as soon as possible?   ✿

8. How soon would you be able to begin to work on this project?

9. Can you give us an idea of what a thing like this might cost?   ✿

10. Why are you interested in this assignment?

11. Have you worked for us before?

12. We observe that your proposal states a time of 20 days, but we are really in a hurry. Will you be able to complete it in, say, 10 days?   ✿

13. Are there any questions that you would like to ask?

14. What do you know about this company?

15. We would really like to engage you for this assignment, but our budget is very limited. Would you be willing to consider something less than the amount quoted in the cost section of your proposal?   ✿

16. We seem to have a problem of high absenteeism. What do you suggest we do about it?   ✿

EFFECTIVE INTERVIEWING

The foregoing sections have provided some guidelines about making the initial interview a success. Clearly, this interview is a two-way interview: you are being interviewed, but you are also interviewing the prospective client. In this final section of the chapter, we discuss some other aspects of effective interviewing.

If the interview is to be effective, you should prepare for it. An important aspect of this preparation involves a careful review of the proposal if one was submitted. Familiarize yourself with the significant details of the proposal before you attend the interview. In the process of preparing for the interview, ask yourself the following questions:

> What is the real purpose of this interview?
> What specific areas and questions should be covered?
> What do I know about the prospective client?

Try to establish a cordial relationship with the prospective client without being too chummy.

During the interview, be sure to listen, and listen, and listen. I have interviewed candidates who, in their eagerness to move on to what they consider to be important, hardly allow you to finish a sentence. Do avoid this mistake. Try to understand the prospective client's problems as they are stated, paying careful attention to any suggestion that the client might make. Answer any questions as fully as possible and always give frank answers.

Prospective clients, like most other human beings, have their biases. You must therefore attempt to separate facts from opinions. For example, a prospective client might tell you that some employees are lazy. That may be an opinion rather than a fact. The fact might be that they are not lazy, but simply not motivated. Given adequate motivation, what appeared to be laziness could rapidly disappear. Opinions are subjective; facts are objective. An independent consultant should always strive for objectivity.

CHAPTER SUMMARY

1. There is a cost to attending an interview. If the total cost of attending an interview exceeds the benefits of attending, then it may not be worth your while to attend.

2. The way you are dressed and groomed and the way you behave at an interview may have significant impact on the outcome of the interview.

3. Rating factors used in interviews include personal appearance, alertness, speech, personality, and manners.

4. The interview serves at least four purposes: (i) it gives the prospective client an opportunity to "size you up" and to explain the details of the assignment; (ii) it gives you the opportunity to verify that you understand the proposed assignment; (iii) it helps you to determine whether you should accept the assignment; and (iv) it gives you the opportunity to collect pertinent data.

5. During the interview, don't allow the client to take unfair advantage of you, don't bite off more than you can chew, and remember to take notes.

6. A Data Form is a useful device that will assist you in gathering pertinent information for the assignment.

7. Listening is important during the interview. By listening, you will gain a great deal of information that may help you to solve your client's problems.

SELF-TEST QUESTIONS

Indicate whether each of the following is true (T) or false (F).

1. _____ An independent consultant should make it a policy to attend all interviews for assignments.

2. _____ The dollar value of a contract, the chances of obtaining the assignment and the cost of attending the interview are all relevant in deciding whether or not to attend the interview.

3. _____ The concept of "expected value" can be used to decide whether or not to attend an interview.

4. _____ You submit a proposal for an assignment for which your fee would be $10,000 if you obtain the assignment. The likelihood of your getting the assignment is 3 out of 10. In that case, the expected value of the assignment is $3,000.

5. _____ Most prospective clients are not at all concerned with the appearance of consultants. Their only interest is in the consultant's ability.

6. _____ If you are well dressed and well groomed, you are likely to make a good first impression on your prospective client.

7. _____ Interviewers usually rate interviewees on appearance, alertness, personality, and manners.

8. _____ It is an effective strategy to attend interviews about five minutes later than the appointed time.

9. _____ When you enter an interview room, you should remain standing until you are invited to sit.

10. _____ The initial consulting interview serves only one purpose, and that is for the prospective client to decide whether or not to engage the services of the consultant.

11. _____ At the initial interview, the independent consultant should try to obtain information on the prospective client's problems and his/her expectations of the consultant, how performance will be measured, and who will be the consultant's main contact.

12. _____ The consultant hopes to leave an interview with an assignment. The consultant should help his/her cause by offering as much free advice as possible.

13. _____ Consultants who offer "free" advice to their clients stand the chance of not getting the assignment.

14. _____ Clients will often attempt to treat consultants as their employees. This

practice should be encouraged by independent consultants.

15. _____ Because of the consultant/client relationship, if a client tries to convince you that he/she has no money, you should immediately reduce your fees in order to accommodate the client.

16. _____ It's generally a bad idea to quote a fee on the spot at a consulting interview.

17. _____ When a prospective client indicates that an interview is over, the consultant should take the cue and leave.

18. _____ The use of a data form to gather information is "amateurish" and should be avoided.

19. _____ A consultant can better prepare for an interview if he/she is familiar with typical questions asked at interviews.

20. _____ At an interview, your objective is irrelevant. The only thing that really matters is the prospective client's opinion.

ANSWERS

1. F   2. F   3. T   4. T   5. F   6. T   7. T   8. F

9. T   10. F   11. T   12. F   13. T   14. T   15. F   16. T

17. T   18. F   19. T   20. F

CHAPTER 10
PLANNING AND CONTROLLING
THE ASSIGNMENT

INTRODUCTION

Independent consultants working alone tend to neglect or minimize the importance of planning and controlling assignments. You want to deliver the best possible service to your clients. Carefully planning and controlling assignments will enhance to quality of your consulting service and help your practice to grow. Planning and controlling assignments are necessary activities for successful independent consulting. Much of the material contained in this chapter applies whether you are working alone or with other consultants under your direction.

The chapter is divided into two parts. The first part deals with planning while the second part deals with controlling. We begin the chapter with a discussion of strategic planning. We then proceed to staffing where we discuss issues that should be considered when assembling the consulting team. A discussion of time planning closes the planning section of the chapter.

The controlling section of the chapter begins with a discussion of the issue of office space for consultants who work at the client organization. We then discuss the importance of keeping an assignment journal and controlling time. We close the chapter with a list of ten questions that will help in controlling assignment quality.

PLANNING THE ASSIGNMENT

Strategic Planning

Once you have been awarded an assignment, it is incumbent upon you to plan and control the assignment in such a way that the work will proceed smoothly and efficiently. Clearly, the amount of planning and controlling necessary will depend upon the nature and complexity of the assignment. An assignment to advise a client on the selection of carpets for a dwelling may not require as much planning and control as an assignment to perform a complete organizational diagnostic analysis for a huge multinational corporation.

To a large extent, if you prepared a proposal for the assignment, you would have already done some strategic planning in terms of outlining the procedure to be followed in performing the assignment, the length of time that it should take, and the staffing of the assignment. Additional information obtained during interviews and briefings will also help to determine:

- when the assignment will begin
- the pace at which the work will proceed

- the order in which segments of the work will be done
- the number and times of interim reports
- the degree of involvement of the client.

Staffing

Assembling the Consulting Team

Assembling the consulting team is an important aspect of planning the assignment. The consulting personnel in a consulting firm will usually consist of people with different interests and different areas of expertise. In assembling the team for an assignment, you must consider the skills required to perform the assignment as well as the expectations and interests of the client.

In assembling the team, you should be careful not to ignore the personalities of the consultants and the client. To the extent that it is possible, the consultant(s) and the client should have matching rather than conflicting personalities. If at all possible, consultants who do not get along with each other should not be assigned to work together on the assignment. When people who do not get along for one reason or another are forced to work together, they may be able to put aside their differences for the good of the project, but if they are unable to do so, the assignment (and the consulting practice) will suffer.

Availability of Personnel

It may often be the case that your firm is handling two or more concurrent assignments involving the same consulting staff. In such circumstances, proper planning is absolutely essential. For example, if a particular consultant is scheduled to begin working on a certain phase of an assignment on a specific date, then you must ensure that the consultant will be available on that date. If he/she has to leave work on another assignment, then the smooth flow of work is interrupted, and efficiency and effectiveness will be sacrificed.

The foregoing example underscores the need for proper planning and scheduling of assignments. Clients may be flexible in terms of the starting dates and completion dates of assignments. If that is the case, then you will have some room for maneuver. If you accept an urgent assignment, you must be sure that you have the staff to deal with it immediately. Remember that your client's interest is paramount.

Time Plan for Assignments

When you accept an assignment, you should carefully consider the whole period necessary for the completion of the assignment. You should refer to the time schedule in your proposal for the starting and final points of the various activities pertaining to the assignment. New consultants may find it difficult to make good estimates of the time required for the completion of certain activities. In this area, as in others, experience will be a good teacher.

In general, you will find that a short assignment requires more detailed time planning than does a long assignment. This is so because you will tend to have greater flexibility with a long assignment. Long assignments appear to be less time-sensitive than short assignments. For this reason, consultants tend to postpone long assignments, or to neglect planning for them. This is a temptation that you will do well to avoid.

Careful time planning will help to keep you on track with your assignments. However, unforeseen events can hamper the scheduled completion of assignments. Proper time planning considers such unforeseen contingencies. In developing a time plan for an assignment, you must consider the role that the client will play in the assignment. If the client does not make his/her input according to the prescribed schedule, then there may be delays and the assignment may not be completed on time. Your time plan must reflect this eventuality.

CONTROLLING THE ASSIGNMENT

So far, we have discussed various aspects of planning an assignment. In the remainder of this chapter, we shall focus on various aspects of controlling an assignment.

Office Space

The problem of office space does not arise if the assignment is executed wholly from the consultant's office. However, many assignments require the consultant to spend a considerable amount of time at the client's premises. If you accept an assignment that requires you to spend several hours at a time at your client's premises, you should make arrangements with the client for suitable accommodation. You will lose valuable consulting time if you have to hunt for office space when you begin the assignment.

Your office at the client's premises does not have to match the elegance of the CEO's office, but it must be adequate and functional. In considering the suitability of office space, remember you are an independent consultant. You will not be highly regarded if you are given only a small table in a corner. Remember that you require a certain amount of privacy for discussions, interviews, and meetings with people in the client organization. Remember also that you will often have sensitive material which is not intended for public display. I was once offered a meeting room from which I was expected to perform my consulting duties for a month. Of course, I informed my client, politely and professionally, that the room was unsuitable for our purposes (his and mine) and requested that other arrangements be made. Within minutes, suitable accommodation was arranged.

Assignment Journal

From the point of view of control, it is of vital importance for the independent consultant to keep a record of activity throughout the assignment. An assignment journal is intended precisely for that purpose. Each evening, the day's significant events are recorded in the assignment journal. Progress made on the assignment, notes written, and relevant telephone calls made should be recorded, with dates, in the assignment journal.

Controlling Time

Whether you are working on the assignment at your office or the client organization, it is necessary to keep an account of the time spent on the assignment. If the assignment is being done at the client organization, acquaint yourself with the working hours and adjust your schedule accordingly. If you need to work long hours at the client organization in order to complete the assignment as scheduled, you should make the necessary arrangements with your client. An Assignment Time Sheet (see Table 10. 1) is a useful device for recording time spent on assignments.

Table 10.1. Assignment Time Sheet

NEW AGE CONSULTING

Assignment Time Sheet

Name of Client _____

Address _____

Consulting Assignment (Subject) _____

Consulting Assignment #_____ Start Date _____
End Date_____

_____

Date   Start Time   End Time   Work Performed No. of Hours

Consultant's Signature_____ Date_____

Day Month Year

_____

Quality Control

If you have junior consultants working on an assignment at the client organization, you must ensure that they are properly supervised. If they are on long-term assignments, it will often be necessary to visit them occasionally to ensure that work is progressing satisfactorily. The dates of such visits should be planned in advance so that adequate preparations involving all parties concerned can be made. You should spend time with your consultants and your client together and separately to assess working relationships and progress on the assignment. If changes need to be made, they should be made as quickly as possible.

Table 10.2 below suggests some questions that may be asked and some areas that may be investigated when attempting to control assignment quality. Let us briefly examine each area of investigation in order.

Question 1 Adequate communication between clients and consultants is extremely important to ensure that the needs of the client are being met. Even though the consulting interview may clarify most of the details pertaining to the assignment, some grey areas may remain. If the consultants fail to communicate with the client, they may end up spending several hours or even days doing something contrary to the desires of the client. The importance of communication between consultants and clients cannot be exaggerated. Some people in the client organization, for a variety of reasons, may develop and demonstrate negative or belligerent attitudes toward the consultants.

Some of them may feel threatened. They may feel that the consultants will reveal weaknesses in their performance and thus offer far less than their full cooperation to the successful completion of the assignment. In these circumstances, the consultants must understand that their main objective is to satisfy the client. They must maintain professionalism as they interact with such uncooperative members of the client organization.

Question 2   Item two in the table deals with progress on the assignment. Regardless of the amount of time and effort devoted to planning the assignment, if it is not carefully monitored, then it is highly unlikely that it will progress according to schedule. Most clients want their jobs completed and delivered as promised in the proposal. It is your responsibility to make sure that the assignment progresses at a rate that is consistent with the planned schedule.

Table 10.2. Quality Control Check

No. Items to be checked	Yes [✓]	No[✓]
1. Is there adequate communication between your consultants and personnel in the client organization?	[ ]	[ ]
2. Is the assignment progressing according to the planned schedule?	[ ]	[ ]
3. Is the client asking the consultants to perform activities outside the terms of the assignment?	[ ]	[ ]
4. Is the assignment journal kept up-to-date and in generally good condition?	[ ]	[ ]
5. Are necessary interim reports being prepared?	[ ]	[ ]
6. Are the consultants still enthusiastic and excited about the assignment?	[ ]	[ ]
7. Are the consultants receiving adequate cooperation from the personnel at the client organization?	[ ]	[ ]
8. Is the client satisfied with the progress of the assignment, and with the working relationship between the consultants and the personnel at the client organization?	[ ]	[ ]
9. Are the consultants maintaining their independence and their objectivity?	[ ]	[ ]
10. Are the fees for the assignment being made by the client as agreed to in the proposal and/or contract?	[ ]	[ ]

Question 3   It is well known among consultants that many clients try to get consultants to do more work than is specified in the agreement. Sometimes, the idea of the extra work is an afterthought generated by the work that is being done. But sometimes it is a simple case of the client trying to take unfair advantage of the consultants. You should not permit this to happen. You should therefore advise your consultants to inform the client that this extra work lies outside the scope of the present assignment and that they would need to obtain permission from their superiors to perform this additional work. If you are the only consultant in your practice, you should point out to the client that the additional work could be accommodated for an additional fee. This usually settles the issue.

Question 4   We turn now to the question of the assignment journal. If the assignment journal is not kept up to date and in good condition, then the information required for the proper control of the current assignment (and future assignments) may be lost entirely. I have always insisted that journal entries be made daily. You should check the entries because they provide you with a great deal of information about what is happening on the assignment and they allow you to make adjustments that may be necessary for the successful completion of the assignment.

Question 5   One of the main purposes (and perhaps the main purpose) of interim reports is to provide information to the client about the progress that is being made on the assignment. They may also serve to justify expenditures that are being made by the client.

Additionally, they tell you, the consultant, how well the assignment is progressing, and allow you to determine whether (and to what extent) adjustments are necessary to complete the assignment on time. Interim reports may also reveal unanticipated problems that require special attention.

Question 6 This question actually forces you to consider the level of morale and motivation of the consultants working on the project. If the consultants do not have the same level of enthusiasm about the assignment as when they began working on it, they will tend to give less than their best, and the client's interest will not be well served. It is important to make sure that a high level of morale is maintained and that the consultants are appropriately motivated to do the best possible job for the client.

Question 7 We have indicated that, for a variety of reasons, the consultants may not receive the full cooperation of the personnel of the client organization. This is a very sensitive issue. People tend to do what seems to be in their self-interest. The uncooperative attitude that may be displayed by personnel in the client organization may stem from insecurity or lack of information. You should approach the uncooperative individuals and inform them that you are there to serve the best interest of the organization, that *they* succeed when the organization succeeds, and that you would really appreciate their cooperation and support. This approach usually produces the desired results. If the uncooperative individuals continue to behave in a manner that will sabotage the assignment, then you have no other option than to bring the matter to your client.

Question 8   It is your responsibility to ensure that the assignment is progressing to the satisfaction of your client and that the working relationships between your consultants and the client are satisfactory.   Early detection of problems makes solutions easier. It is not a good idea to wait until the completion of an assignment to find out that your client is not satisfied with what you have   done.   Sending   consultants   to   the   client organization is somewhat of an intrusion into the normal and customary working relationships at the client organization. You should check with your client to make sure that performing the assignment is not causing *unnecessary* disruption.

Question 9   When consultants work for an extended period at the client organization, they may become too close to problems within the client organization to understand all the ramifications. This may reduce their ability to bring fresh insight to problems. There is also a tendency for clients to react to them as their *employees*. You must be sure that your consultants are maintaining their independence and their objectivity.

Question 10   This last item in Table 10.2 must be handled skillfully and tactfully.   If the client is not paying the fees, then the matter must be discussed. A tactful reminder is often sufficient. If payment is still not made, then it may be possible to make alternative payment arrangements. After that, if the client still does not pay, then it may be necessary to discontinue work on the assignment.

Support of Consultants

If you employ other consultants in your consulting firm, you must remember that they need to feel that they are a part of the firm. They need to be encouraged and supported on assignments. They need to feel that they are valuable members of a team. You must demonstrate, by words and deed, that your interest in your consulting staff extends beyond the fees they bring in. Do remember that the quality of every consulting assignment is affected by the support and encouragement given to your consulting staff.

CHAPTER SUMMARY

1. Planning and controlling an assignment will help to ensure that the work progresses smoothly and efficiently. Some assignments require greater planning and control than others.

2. Strategic planning of an assignment involves determining when the assignment will begin, the pace at which the work will proceed, the order in which segments of the work will be done, the number and frequency of interim reports, and the degree of involvement of the client.

3. Each consulting assignment has to be staffed. The skills of the consultants must be matched with the skills required to perform the assignment, and care must be taken to avoid personality clashes between consultants and clients.

4. Care must also be taken to ensure that assignments are scheduled in such a way that consultants will be available to work on assignments.

5. In planning the time for the completion of assignments, you should make provisions for unforeseen contingencies.

6. If the assignment has to be performed at the premises of the client, you must make arrangements for suitable office space.

7. It is a good idea to keep an assignment journal in which you record a summary of each day's significant events — progress made on the assignment, notes written, telephone calls made, etc. It is important to record dates.

8. The independent consultant's time is valuable, and must therefore be controlled. As a control device, you should keep an account of the time spent on each assignment.

9. To control the quality of work, you should pay attention to certain quality control items. If deficiencies are detected, they should be rectified as quickly as possible.

10. Support and encouragement of independent consultants on assignments will help to maintain the quality of work on assignments.

SELF-TEST QUESTIONS

Indicate whether each of the following is true (T) or false (F).

1. _____ If you have done a good job at preparing a proposal, then there is not much additional benefit from planning the assignment that results from that proposal.

2. _____ All assignments require the same amount of planning and controlling, regardless of their complexity.

3. _____ The fact that you have carefully prepared a proposal means that you have already done some strategic planning for the assignment.

4. _____ Strategic planning involves determining when the assignment will begin, the pace at which it will proceed, and the order in which segments of the work will be performed.

5. _____ In assembling the team for an assignment, the consultant should consider the skills required to perform the assignment but not the personalities of the members of the team.

6. _____ The flexibility of clients in terms of starting dates and completion dates gives the consultant some flexibility in planning and scheduling assignments.

7. _____ In estimating the time required to complete an assignment, the consultant should refer to the time schedule in the proposal for the starting and final points of the various activities pertaining to the assignment.

8. _____ In general, a long assignment requires more detailed time planning than does a short assignment.

9. _____ If you do your time planning properly, there will be no need to make allowance for unforeseen contingencies.

10. _____ You do not have to worry about suitable office space if you are working at the client organization because the client takes care of that.

11. _____ In order to maintain your prestige as an independent consultant, you must make sure that your office at the client organization is at least as elegant as the CEO's office.

12. _____ As long as you do a good job, the type of space you use at the client organization is irrelevant.

13. _____ If a client offers you space that is inappropriate for consulting purposes, you should not accept it.

14. _____ An assignment journal helps the consultant control the assignment.

15. _____ Even if you are working on an assignment at your office, it is still necessary to keep an account of the time spent on the assignment.

16. _____ If you have junior consultants working on an assignment at the client organization, you should avoid visiting them unannounced.

17. _____ Regardless of the amount of time and effort devoted to planning the assignment, if it is not carefully monitored, then it is highly unlikely that it will progress according to schedule.

18. _____ Interim reports tell the consultant how well the assignment is progressing.

19. _____ Consultants are professionals. They will therefore not become so close to problems that they cannot understand all the ramifications.

20. _____ Once you have agreed to accept an assignment, you must complete it even if the client does not pay.

ANSWERS

1. F   2. F   3. T   4. T   5. F   6. T   7. T   8. F

9. F   10. F   11. F   12. F   13. T   14. T   15. T   16. T

17. T   18. T   19. F   20. F

CHAPTER 11
MANAGING A CONSULTING BUSINESS

INTRODUCTION

In this chapter, we shall study some aspects of managing a consulting business. Some aspects of running a consulting business have been discussed in previous chapters. For example, we have studied marketing and pricing of consulting services, as well as proposal and report writing. In this chapter, we shall focus on four aspects of managing a consulting business:

- Forms of business organization
- Records and accounts
- Planning for profit
- Insurance

Other aspects such as human resource management and financing are important even though they are not discussed in this chapter.

We begin the chapter with a discussion of the various forms of business organization from which the consultant can choose. The advantages and disadvantages of the single proprietorship, the partnership, and the corporation will receive due attention. Good business management requires that independent consultants keep accurate records of their business transactions. After discussing the various forms of business organization, we take a look at certain records and accounts that the independent consultant should keep. We then discuss how the independent consultant can plan for profit, the use of computers by independent consultants, and end the chapter with an examination of the role of insurance in the consultant's business.

FORMS OF BUSINESS ORGANIZATION

Our main concern in this section of the chapter is to consider the various ways in which an independent consultant can organize his/her business. If you have already established a consulting practice, you may have already decided on the form of business organization that is appropriate for your business. Nevertheless, it is a good idea to be aware of the various types of business organizations and their characteristics. The information will help you to determine the most appropriate form for your consulting business.

The Single Proprietorship

The single proprietorship is a form of business organization in which the enterprise is owned by a single individual. If you are the sole owner of your consulting business, then it is a single (sole) proprietorship. You may operate your consulting practice with the assistance of relatives, or friends or with one or more paid employees such as a receptionist/secretary and a clerk. But you are the only person who is legally responsible for the firm's debts, and only you are entitled to the firm's profits.

Advantages and Disadvantages of a Single Proprietorship

Advantages The advantages of the single proprietorship include:

1. Single proprietors derive a certain amount of satisfaction, self-pride, and independence from owning their own businesses. You can sense the feeling of pride and accomplishment when someone proudly states, "I own my own business."

2. Knowing that they can lose all their possessions if their businesses fail, single proprietors are likely to make special efforts to run their businesses efficiently.

3. In situations demanding swift action, single proprietorships enjoy a considerable advantage over other forms of business organization, since owners do not need to consult with or seek the agreement of anyone other than themselves.

4. Single proprietors are likely to be more concerned about developing good working relations with the few employees they may have, and with securing the goodwill of their clients. If single proprietors are successful, the quality of their services will be high, and the effect on their revenues favorable.

5. Single proprietors may enjoy tax benefits. The earnings of single proprietors are subject to tax once

only. We will see later that corporations do not enjoy this advantage.

Disadvantages Among the disadvantages of the single proprietorship are:

1. Single proprietors are at a distinct disadvantage in situations requiring huge capital outlays. Not many single proprietors are in a position to raise the large sums of money required in many of today's modern businesses. Hence, we do not find many single proprietors owning very large business firms.

2. The single proprietorship form of business organization suffers from uncertainty about the continuation of the business in the event of the death or retirement of the owner. It must be observed, however, that some single proprietorships have been known to survive through several generations in the hands of the same family.

3. The biggest disadvantage of the single proprietorship, however, is the fact that the owners are legally responsible for all debts incurred by their businesses. Single proprietors are not protected by limited liability. This means that if their businesses fail, single proprietors are fully liable and can lose personal assets such as cars, furniture, or even homes since, in this form of business organization, there is no legal distinction between personal assets and business assets.

Partnership

A partnership is a form of business organization in which two or more people pool their physical, financial, and human resources to form and operate a business enterprise. If you decide to enter into a partnership arrangement (perhaps with one or more consultants) you should draw up a *partnership agreement*. Such an agreement usually contains:

- the name of the business
- the purpose of the business
- the contribution to be made by each partner
- the distribution of profits among the partners.

Other matters such as place of business, responsibilities of each partner, and the duration of the partnership may also be covered by the partnership agreement.

The partnership may be a general partnership or a limited partnership. In a general partnership, the partners are not only jointly liable for the debts of the partnership but in addition, are jointly and severally liable. Each partner can bind the partnership irrespective of the consent of the other partners. A limited partnership is composed of one or more general partners who conduct the business, and one or more persons who contribute an amount in actual cash, called limited partners. A limited partner is liable to the firm or to its creditors only to the extent of the capital he/she has agreed to contribute, and no more. Limited partners share in the profits of the partnership according to the partnership agreement, but they do not take any part in the management of the firm.

Advantages and Disadvantages of the Partnership

Advantages   The following are the major advantages of the partnership:

1. The partnership has the ability to raise more capital than the single proprietorship can raise.

2. The partnership, like the single proprietorship, is not subject to tax. Individual partners, of course, pay taxes on their incomes, but the business itself pays no tax on its earnings.

3. Discussion is likely to take place among the partners before any important action is taken. These discussions are likely to lead to more sober decisions than those reached by single proprietors who do not need to engage in such discussions. According to the adage, two heads are better than one.

4. The partnership may benefit from the variety of special talents and skills possessed by the partners. One may have expertise in marketing, another in management, another in accounting, etc., all contributing to the successful operation of the business.

Disadvantages   The partnership suffers from the following disadvantages:

1. The partnership lacks continuity. If one partner dies or if agreement cannot be reached among the partners, the partnership may have to be dissolved.

2. Although the partnership may be able to raise more capital than the single proprietorship, it is still severely limited in the amount of funds it can raise.

3. There is the danger that some of the partners may be incompetent or lack good judgment. This can spell disaster for a consulting firm that must hold the confidence of its clients. Remember that the success of a consulting business depends significantly on its ability to project an image of efficiency and credibility.

4. The partnership does not have limited liability. This is probably its most serious drawback. Each member is fully liable to the extent of his or her personal possessions for any debts incurred by the business. Limited partners are liable only to the extent of their investment in the business. It is possible for one partner to make a bad business decision in the name of the partnership, thus jeopardizing the financial security of the other partners, since they are severally and jointly liable.

The Corporation

Of all the forms of business organization, the corporation is the most complex. It is a separate legal entity distinct from the shareholders who own it. The capital of the corporation is raised by issuing (selling) shares of stocks to persons who wish to become part owners of the company. The corporation is owned by its shareholders. Owning a share entitles the shareholder to a certain portion of any profits which may be distributed by the management.

The corporation is governed by a board of directors elected by the shareholders at the annual meetings. Sometimes a special meeting is called for this purpose.

The board appoints members to fill any vacancies that may occur between annual meetings due to the resignation or death of elected members, and these appointees hold office until the next annual meeting.

Advantages and Disadvantages of the Corporation

Advantages   The corporation has several advantages:

1. It has a tremendous ability to raise huge amounts of money. The shares of the corporation can easily be transferred from one owner to another. If you hold shares in a corporation, you can sell your shares to someone who is willing to buy them.

2. This form of business organization has the continuity that is lacking in the single proprietorship and the partnership. If a shareholder dies, the corporation continues as usual.

3. The corporation can usually afford to hire the services of experts. It can hire a staff of researchers, economists, top management personnel, accountants, lawyers, and experts in other fields.

4. In a corporation, each owner (shareholder) is liable only to the extent of his/her investment in the business. That is, the owners have *limited liability*. If the company fails, each shareholder's liability is limited to the amount of money spent in buying shares in the business. This is undoubtedly one of the greatest advantages of the corporation.

Disadvantages   The following are the disadvantages of the corporation:

1. The earnings of the corporation are taxed twice. The corporation pays tax before its profits are distributed, and the shareholders also pay tax on their dividends.

2. The shareholders may have little or no control over the corporation, and those who make the day-to-day decisions of the corporation may not have the same incentives as the owners.

3. The size of the corporation often forces a wedge between labor and management and also destroys the close personal relationship between owner and client that is typical of the single proprietorship.

Note: From the point of view of clients, the partnership is ideal for a consulting firm. If one consultant does a poor job, it exposes the other consultants as well to any unfavorable consequences. The reputation of the entire consulting firm may be tarnished. This is a sort of safety net that ensures each consultant in the firm will do his/her best to see that the best decisions are made. It provides an incentive for consultation among the consultants, which is definitely a great advantage to the firm's clients.

RECORDS AND ACCOUNTS

One of the essential factors in running a successful consulting practice is the maintenance of proper records and accounts. If you have no knowledge of bookkeeping or accounting, it is well to hire the services of someone who does, so that he/she can set up and maintain an accounting and record-keeping system for you. Although a good record-keeping system will not, by itself, guarantee business success, it will keep you informed and make you aware of the status of your consulting practice and reveal weaknesses in operation which, if not detected and attended to, might have serious consequences.

Laws and regulations require that certain information be filed with the government. For example, income tax returns are required by the government, and this provides a great incentive for keeping business records. However, accurate records are required for proper business decision-making. For most independent consultants, an elaborate and complicated record-keeping system is probably unnecessary. The important point to consider is that the system should be appropriate for *your* consulting business. For example, if you do not have any employees, you do not need to set up payroll accounting. Similarly, if you do not keep inventories, you do not need to account for them.

Accounting Records

A session with a competent accountant will help to determine what types of accounting records you need. But it is safe to say that you will need to keep track of services to clients, you need records of your expenses, and you need to keep records of important letters, contracts, proposals, etc.

Although a single-entry system may be used by some relatively small consulting firms because of its simplicity, it has the disadvantage that it records transactions in one place only. On the other hand, the double entry system requires that each transaction be recorded in two places. This system provides more information and allows for greater control.

Two important accounting books are the *Journal* and the *Ledger*. The journal or the day book is the original book of entry, and it records the daily transactions in chronological order. Similar items in the journal are entered either individually or as totals in ledger accounts. Because of the double-entry system, the ledger accounts must balance.

In order to illustrate how accounting information may be recorded, we shall consider the following transactions:

- sales of services
- cash transactions
- accounts receivable
- accounts payable
- expenses

Sales

Your income is derived from the sale of consulting services to your clients. It is important that you keep a record of each sale made. Information on sales is recorded in a *sales journal*. It should include the date of the transaction, the description of the sale, and the amount of the sale. An analysis of the sales journal provides information that can be used for future planning. It also keeps you informed of sales trends and helps you to keep track of your revenues.

Cash

If cash is not properly handled, losses can easily occur. Payment for most consulting services is usually made by cheque. However, depending on your area of consulting, some clients may pay cash for your services. The recording system for cash should be designed to minimize losses. Cheques and cash are handled together. Your recording system should provide for the identification of each person who presents a cheque. For most independent consultants, payment by cheque does not present a problem mainly because of the nature of the interaction between the consultant and the client. The situation is not like a customer walking off the street, purchasing an item and paying by cheque.

It is good business practice to make all payments by cheque. However, it is inconvenient to make very small payments by cheque. In such circumstances, payment by cash is more economical. An updated checkbook is a useful device for keeping track of your cash position. By adding deposits and subtracting each cheque on the checkbook stub, the checkbook becomes an account ledger. Each cheque is entered in the *cash journal* to indicate the account to which it is charged.

It is a good idea to establish a *petty cash fund* to pay small bills such as postage stamps, and occasional taxi fares. Each payment from petty cash should be recorded on a form to keep track of the account and the amount paid. The total amount on the petty cash form plus the amount of cash remaining in the petty cash fund should always be equal to the total amount established for the fund. A cheque is written periodically to replenish the fund, and the expenditures recorded are transferred to the proper accounts in the cash journal.

Accounts Receivable

Because of the billing practices in the consulting business, consultants usually have some amounts of money owing to them. These are *accounts receivable*. The "accounts receivable" account records transactions for which payment will be received at a future date. Periodically, each client's account is totaled and an invoice is sent to the client according to the payment arrangement made. As payments are received, the amounts of the cheque are recorded in each client's account and totaled for entry in the sales and cash receipts journal.

An analysis of the accounts receivable records provides information that is necessary for managerial decision-making and control. For example, it reveals which clients are in arrears and which accounts need special attention. Obviously, the more clients you have, the greater the need for accounts receivable records.

Accounts Payable

In the process of operating your consulting business, you incur some debt obligations. For example, you may have loan payments, telephone and electricity bills, rent, taxes, wages, and so on. These obligations are *accounts payable*. Such transactions are recorded in a *cash disbursements journal*. Virtually all these payments will be made by cheque.

It is a good practice to organize invoices and bills according to the due date. It is practical to include a "miscellaneous" column in the cash disbursements journal for occasional (as opposed to regular monthly) payments. You would provide special columns for regular monthly payments such as rent, wages, and utilities. An item such as the purchase of a printer is usually an occasional purchase and could be handled in the miscellaneous column.

Expenses

Various types of expenses are incurred in running a consulting business. You purchase supplies, you buy insurance, and your office machines suffer depreciation over time. You purchase a postage stamp today and you use it today. You purchase a filing cabinet today but you will use it for several years in the future. The bases of payments for the costs of operating your consulting business vary from daily to over an extended time. An accurate assessment of your net income can be made only by determining revenues and expenses for the same time.

There are two bases for computing profit or net income: the *accrual basis* and the *cash basis*. On the accrual basis, adjustments must be made to align revenues and expenses. On the cash basis, items are charged as they are actually paid. A vital assumption of the cash basis is that payments and use occur in the same period. Some jurisdictions specify which basis must be used in certain circumstances. In the absence of such stipulations, most independent consultants opt for the cash basis mainly because of its simplicity.

Financial Statements

The information that you have compiled in your records will enable you to produce financial statements. You need to be aware of the financial position of your consulting business at any given time. It is equally important for you to be able to determine whether your business operations are resulting in profits or losses and to know the magnitudes of these figures. The balance sheet and the income statement will provide information about your firm's financial position and operations.

THE BALANCE SHEET

The *balance sheet* presents a summary of the financial position of the business at a particular date, showing assets, liabilities, and net worth or equity. *Assets* are the physical, financial, and other things of value that your firm owns. These include such items as cash, accounts receivable, office equipment and furniture, etc. *Liabilities* are the debts of the business and include such items as bills to be paid, bank loans, and mortgages. *Net worth* is the difference between total assets and total liabilities. Table 11.1 illustrates a balance sheet for a hypothetical consulting firm. Let us examine it.

Assets

In the "assets" section, assets are classified as *current assets* and *fixed assets*. Current assets are those that are likely to be turned into cash within a year. Fixed assets are those that are long-lived and tangible. They include items such as equipment, buildings, and land.

Current Assets include items such as cash, accounts receivable, and prepaid expenses. *Cash* includes cash on hand and deposits in your checking account in the bank. You must keep a part of your assets in the form of cash so that you can pay current bills. However, since cash is a noninterest-earning asset, it is uneconomical to keep too much cash.

Table 11.1. **Example of a Balance Sheet**

New Age Consulting
Balance Sheet
December 31, 20

ASSETS

Current Assets:	
Cash	$ 3,000
Accounts receivable	20,000
Prepaid expenses	500
Total Current Assets	23,500
Fixed Assets:	
Equipment	12,000
Furniture	4,000
Less reserve for depreciation	1,500
Net fixed assets	14,500
Total Assets	**38,000**

LIABILITIES

Current Liabilities:	
Accounts payable	$ 5,000
Bank loans	10,000
Total Current Liabilities	15,000
Long Term	3,000
Total Liabilities	**18,000**
Net Worth (Equity)	20,000
Liabilities + Net Worth	**38,000**

Accounts receivable result from extending credit to your clients. The accounts receivable figure represents the total of all balances owing to you by your clients at the date of the balance sheet. You can structure your billing policy in such a way that only a part of your total fee for an assignment is unpaid while you are working on the assignment.

Prepaid expenses are expenses for items that are paid for in advance of their use. The items are expected to be used up within a relatively short period. Prepaid expenses include prepaid insurance and office supplies. They usually represent only a small percentage of the current assets.

Fixed assets are tangible assets that are relatively durable (lasting more than a year) and used in your consulting firm's operation. Examples of fixed assets are computers, printers, photocopy machines, laminating machines, furniture, and binding machines.

Liabilities

Liabilities are classified as *current liabilities* and *long-term liabilities*.

Current Liabilities are debt obligations that are payable within a year out of current assets. Current liabilities include items such as notes payable, accounts payable, interest payable, and taxes payable.

Long-term Liabilities are debt obligations that are not due and payable until after one year. Long-term liabilities include items such as notes payable (due more than one year after the date of the balance sheet, and mortgages.

Analysis of the Balance Sheet

The balance sheet provides information that is useful for managerial decision-making. The most convenient way of using this information is to examine balance sheet ratios. Numerous ratios can be calculated from the balance sheet, but the current ratio is one of the most important of these ratios. The current ratio tells how many times the current liabilities could be paid with the current assets. It indicates the extent to which the business can meet its current obligations. The current ratio is calculated using the following formula:

$$\text{Current Ratio} = \frac{\text{Current Assets}}{\text{Current Liabilities}}$$

A current ratio of 2:1 is usually considered satisfactory. In considering the current ratio, you should also pay some attention to the amount of cash available to meet cash requirements within a given period.

THE INCOME STATEMENT

You (the independent consultant) and others with an interest in your consulting business would want to know how much profit was made from operations during a period of time. You would want to know whether or not your consulting practice was profitable. You would want to know your revenues and expenses from operating the business. This information is contained in your *Income Statement* or your *Profit and Loss Statement* as it is also called. The Income Statement shows revenues, expenses, and profits for a certain period. Table 11.2 illustrates an Income Statement for a hypothetical consulting firm.

You should prepare Income Statements on a regular basis (perhaps monthly) in order to provide regular information about the margin of profit that your consulting business is currently making and to track the trend of such profits. In this way, you will be able to take immediate action if the profit margin is falling below what you consider to be a satisfactory percentage of profit (income) from your business operations.

Planning Your Profit (Income)

Income from your consulting practice should not be regarded as a chance occurrence. The independent consultant should realize that he/she can plan for profit. In this section, we show you how you can plan effectively for profit. By planning for profit, the consultant avoids viewing income as nothing but a leftover that he/she cannot affect. We will study how you can plan your operations in such a way that you earn the income that you can reasonably expect from your consulting business.

Table 11.2. **Example of an Income Statement**

New Age Consulting
Income Statement
January 1 to December 31, 20

Revenue:

Income from fees	$90,000
Other income	2,000
Total Revenue	$92,000

Expenses:

Salaries	$20,000
Rent	5,000
Telephone	4,000
Supplies	3,000
Postage	2,000
Advertising	10,000
Travel and accommodation	3,000
Printing	500
Insurance	500
Miscellaneous expenses	500
Total Expenses	**$48,500**

Net Income	$43,500

FIVE STEPS TO PROFIT (INCOME) PLANNING

The following steps indicate the process of planning your income.

Step 1: **Establish Your Income Objective**

As an independent consultant, you must be able to determine what is a *reasonable* income that you should make from your consulting business. The emphasis on "reasonable" suggests that estimates must be realistic. Your estimate of your desired income may be based on considerations such as the annual income you could have earned as an employee, the interest income you could have earned on the money you invested in your business, and the number of hours you devote to operating your business.

Let us assume, for example, that you would receive a salary of $45,000 per year working for someone else. Let us assume further that you have invested $10,000 in your business and that you could have earned 6% interest on this money if it were placed in a savings account. With this information, you could establish a realistic income objective of $45,600. This figure could be adjusted according to the number of hours you plan to spend at your practice.

Step 2: Determine Your Expected Revenue

The estimate of your expected revenue cannot be pulled out of a magician's hat. It should be based on factors such as general economic trends, the market for your consulting services, trends in your past revenues, your marketing and promotional activities, etc. With this kind of information, you will be able to estimate your revenue for the year. Let us assume that on the basis of the information that you have collected, you can figure out that you could increase your revenues by 10% over last year's figure. If your total revenue for last year was $92,000, then your estimated revenue for the next year will be $101,200 (i.e., $92,000 x 1.10).

Step 3: Estimate the Expenses Necessary to Generate Your Target Revenue

This step requires that you collect expense data for the past year, at least, and then estimate the value of each expense item, making appropriate adjustments. Table 11.3 illustrates the process.

Table 11.3. Estimate of Expenses

Expense Item	Actual Last Year	Estimated 20--
Salaries	$20,000	$21,000
Rent	5,000	5,000
Telephone	4,000	4,500
Supplies	3,000	3,200
Postage	2,000	1,800
Advertising	10,000	10,500
Travel and accommodation	3,000	3,500
Printing	500	600
Insurance	500	600
Miscellaneous	500	600
Total	**$48,500**	**$51,300**

Step 4: Compute Your Estimated Income from the Figures Determined from Steps 2 and 3

On the basis of the information derived from Steps 2 and 3, the estimated income is:

$$\$101{,}200 - \$51{,}300 = \$49{,}900$$

By comparing this income figure with last year's, we note that it is $6,400 more, or an increase of 14.7 per cent over last year's income of $43,500.

Step 5: Compare Your Estimated Income with Your Desired Income

The estimated income of $49,900 is $4,300 more than the $45,600 income objective that has been established. If the estimated income was inadequate to satisfy the desired goal, then you would consider some alternatives such as reducing planned expenses, changing your consulting fee, increasing your planned client base by, for example, considering more effective advertising or by improving your company's image. Perhaps you may also need to review your income goal to see if it is realistic. If it is not realistic, it should be revised.

THE USE OF COMPUTERS

I would venture to state as a fact, that most independent consultants now use personal computers in their practices. This author remembers conditions in the consulting business when proposals and reports had to be written on typewriters. It was arduous work, and the result was a far cry from the kinds of documents that we can now produce with a computer word processing program. An independent consultant who claims to be incapable of running his/her consulting business without a computer is probably not exaggerating. Computers are literally indispensable for many consultants.

Proposal and Report Writing

In Chapters 7 and 8, we discussed proposal and report writing. We stressed the importance of professional-looking work. Computer word processing programs allow consultants to present great-looking proposals and reports, complete with color printing if required. Print enhancements such as bold, italics, underlining, and different fonts (letter sizes and styles) are all available in computer word processing programs. These programs easily and quickly check your documents for spelling accuracy. They will also help you with synonyms and antonyms, and you can embellish your documents with a variety of graphic images.

Database

A database program is quite useful. It is a program that helps you store data in a manner that is appropriate for your particular purpose. For example, you can use a database program for the names and addresses of your clients and prospective clients. You can use it to generate mailing lists and mailing labels, and it can sort your data alphabetically, geographically, chronologically, by sex, or by other desired characteristics. Clearly, many independent consultants will find many important uses for a database program.

Spreadsheet

You can use a spreadsheet program to perform a variety of mathematical and statistical calculations. Many of them have graph-producing capabilities. For example, many spreadsheets can generate bar graphs, pie charts, and line graphs quite easily, and these can then be imported into your documents created with your word processing programs.

Accounting Packages

Earlier in this chapter, we discussed accounting and record keeping. In that discussion, we focused on what is now referred to as "manual" accounting. Many good computerized accounting programs can easily handle accounting and other record-keeping functions for your consulting firm. These software packages allow you to enter accounting data in a way that permits you to keep track of all types of transactions. With a few clicks on the mouse and a few keyboard strokes, you can generate financial statements painlessly. And when it is time to prepare your income tax returns, computer programs can also be used for that purpose.

The Internet and the World Wide Web

Consulting and information are inseparable. It is largely a result of the kind of information you have that you are an independent consultant. That is what makes you an expert. It has often been said that we are living in the information age. The computer is a device that links us to this vast information bank. Information on just about anything is available on the Internet. If you are "connected", you can easily inform yourself so that you can better serve your clients. The World Wide Web opens up a tremendous opportunity for you to market your consulting services. An appropriate web page could boost your consulting practice, and an e-mail address provides another means whereby your clients and prospective clients can reach you.

Overall Increases in Productivity

The use of computers enables the independent consultant to produce professional proposals and reports quickly. Database programs allow you to keep track of, and manage an incredible amount of data. Spreadsheet programs are fabulous for split-second calculations, and accounting programs help you to keep track of your company's financial position and operations. Because of the speed with which you can accomplish all these functions with computers, their use greatly increases the efficiency and the overall productivity of the independent consultant. If you are not computerized, consider what a computer might be able to do for you.

INSURANCE

Independent consultants, like other business people, are exposed to a variety of risks. Insurance enables you to effectively safeguard your business assets from losses that can result from these risks. It is a smart decision to use insurance to minimize your losses. The importance of insurance becomes evident when you consider what would happen to your consulting practice if any of the following occurred.

(a) Fire destroys your office furniture and equipment

(b) A thief breaks into your office and takes off with your computers, photocopy machine, fax machine, and other office equipment

(c) A client injures his/her leg after tripping over an extension chord in your office and is awarded a liability judgment of $12,000

(d) Your office leaks during heavy rainfall and causes severe damage to your furniture and important documents.

Incidents of this nature can be a tremendous setback to an independent consultant who is not adequately protected by insurance. To operate your consulting practice without any kind of insurance at all is to flirt with disaster.

Types of Insurance Coverage

There are many types of insurance coverage, and insurance brokers and agents are ready and eager to sell you any of a variety of insurance. It does not make good economic sense to attempt to insure your consulting business against every conceivable risk. The premiums that you would have to pay would exceed the benefits from such coverage. However, in buying insurance coverage, you should consider, in addition to the protection of your assets, the peace of mind and freedom from worry that insurance provides.

Typically, an independent consultant would consider the following types of insurance:

- Property
- Liability
- Theft, Robbery and Burglary

Protection of Property

The main type of insurance in this category is probably fire insurance. Depending on the jurisdiction, a standard fire insurance policy may insure you only for fire, lightning, and losses resulting from the temporary removal of assets from your office because of fire. This basic coverage may be broadened by endorsements to include landslides, falling objects, broken glasses, broken water and heating systems, and other such damages to property.

Liability Insurance

If one of your consultants, your receptionist, or some other employee in your office is injured because of negligence or carelessness on your part, you may be liable for damages. Workers' Compensation may be applicable in some jurisdictions. You will be able to protect yourself against liability for injury to your employees while they are engaged in their duties.

You are responsible for injury or damage to persons or property of others that is due to your negligence. You can protect yourself against damage claims brought against you by purchasing liability insurance. A policy may be arranged to cover all liability risks in connection with the operation of your business, subject to a few exclusions. If you do not require such a comprehensive liability policy, you can obtain one that is tailored to your specific needs. For example, you could obtain a policy that covers tenants' liability, professional liability, and contractual liability.

Theft, Robbery and Burglary Insurance

Theft is defined as the stealing of your property. If someone steals your fax machine while it is unprotected, the loss is classified as theft. *Robbery* entails depriving you of your property by violence or the threat of violence. If you were just about to leave your office to go to your bank to make a deposit, and someone holds you up at gunpoint and relieves you of your cash, such a loss would be classified as robbery. *Burglary* is the forcible entry of your premises. If someone breaks down your office door to gain entry into your office and steals your computer, that loss would be classified as burglary. Clearly, these losses can seriously affect your consulting practice. Insurance can provide protection against such losses.

A Final Word On Insurance

In the final section of this chapter, we have studied what we consider to be some relevant aspects of insurance. Insurance is a very complex matter and we have attempted to make you aware of what insurance can do for your consulting business.

We have examined only a small fraction of the various types of insurance. It is unlikely that you will need all the different types of insurance that are available, or that you will be able to afford them if you want them. Since insurance costs money, and since you do not have unlimited financial resources, choosing the types of insurance that are of greatest importance to your consulting business is a matter that requires you to exercise good judgment.

The careful planning and selection of insurance is a necessary step in managing a consulting business for success. Adequate protection by insurance coverage significantly reduces the risk of business failure, relieves you of needless worry, and gives you peace of mind. It allows you to focus more on satisfying your clients' needs.

CHAPTER SUMMARY

1. Major forms of business organization are the single proprietorship, the partnership, and the corporation. Each has advantages and disadvantages. The greatest disadvantage of the single proprietorship and the partnership is the lack of limited liability. Limited liability is the greatest advantage of the corporation.

2. If a partnership is formed, a partnership agreement should be drawn up, specifying the name of the business, the purpose for which the business is formed, the contribution of each partner, and the distribution of profits among the partners.

3. Records of business transactions are important. They help you to keep track of what is happening in your business. They allow you to detect weaknesses that may cause problems. The journal and the ledger are particularly important.

4. The Balance Sheet and the Income Statement contain a great deal of information about your consulting business. By analyzing them, you will be kept aware of your assets, liabilities, net worth, revenues, expenses and profits.

5. You should actually plan your income from your consulting business, rather than accepting it as a factor over which you have no control.

6. The use of a computer in your consulting business can increase your efficiency and productivity.

7. You can protect your assets and minimize losses by purchasing adequate insurance coverage.

SELF-TEST QUESTIONS

Indicate whether each of the following is true (T) or false (F).

1. _____ The single proprietorship form of business organization exists where there is a single firm in a particular industry.

2. _____ In a single proprietorship, the owner must manage his/her business without the help of any employees.

3. _____ The only important advantage that single proprietors enjoy is that they are protected by limited liability.

4. _____ In a single proprietorship, the owner is legally responsible for all debts incurred by his/her business.

5. _____ Each partner in a partnership is exempt from personal income tax.

6. _____ A corporation is formed when two or more partnerships decide to merge and become one big business organization.

7. _____ Since a corporation has limited liability, it cannot be held liable for any debts that its managers may incur while doing busines in the name of the corporation.

8. _____ A corporation is owned by its shareholders.

9. _____ Accurate accounting and record-keeping are important in large corporations and retail outlets, but they are not that important for independent consultants.

10. _____ Every consulting business needs to keep records of services performed for clients, expenses incurred, income, proposals submitted, and engagements obtained.

11. _____ A single-entry system of accounts is simple, but it does not allow as much control as a double-entry system.

12. _____ Daily transactions are recorded in the journal in chronological order.

13. _____ One advantage of the double-entry system of accounts is that each transaction must be recorded in two places, thus the ledger accounts do not have to balance.

14. _____ The only records that an independent consultant really needs are records of income and expenses so that a proper tax return can be filed.

15. _____ As an independent consultant, you should insist on payment by cash because from an accounting stand point, control is much easier when payment is made by cash.

16. _____ Cheques received are not entered in the cash journal because cheques and cash are not handled together.

17. _____ The total amount on a petty cash form, together with the amount of cash remaining in the petty cash fund should always be equal to the total amount of the fund.

18. _____ Accounts receivable refer to the amount of money the consultant has received from clients as of a particular date.

19. _____ Accounts payable should be recorded in a cash disbursement journal.

20. _____ Most independent consultants would tend to operate on a cash basis (as opposed to an accrual basis) because of the relative simplicity of the cash basis.

21. _____ A balance sheet contains information about assets, liabilities and net worth of an entity.

22. _____ As far as independent consulting is concerned, the item referred to as "accounts receivable" constitutes an important liability item.

23. _____ As long as independent consultants are paid upon completion of assignments, they never have accounts receivable.

24. _____ The amount of accounts receivable that a consultant has depends partly on how he/she structures his/her billing policy.

25. _____ The current ratio is defined as current assets divided by current liabilities.

26. _____ The current ratio is an indication of the extent to which the enterprise can meet its current liabilities.

27. _____ A consulting business is in a sound financial position as long as current liabilities exceed its current assets, resulting in a current ratio greater than 1.

28. _____ The income statement is a record of revenues, expenses and net income during a certain period of time.

29. _____ Given the nature of the independent consulting business, there is no need for independent consultants to prepare income statements more often than once a year.

30. _____ As long as an independent consultant establishes a profit goal and plans his/her operation properly, the profit goal will be reached.

31. _____ The independent consultant must accept that profit is a residual — the difference between total revenue and total expenses, and that not much can be done about it.

32. _____ In establishing income, the consultant must consider not only the salary that he/she could have earned as an employee.

33. _____ In establishing an estimate of expected revenue for any given year, the consultant must ignore the revenues for previous years because they are irrelevant.

34. _____ The use of computers in consulting cannot really affect the consultant's efficiency. Only training and experience can do that.

35. _____ Insurance can be used to minimize your losses.

36. _____ It is usually an unwise decision to operate a consulting practice without any insurance.

37. _____ If the consultant can afford it, he/she should purchase whatever insurance is available for his/her consulting practice.

38. _____ If estimated income fails to satisfy desired income, the only alternative available is to revise the income goal.

39. _____ An increase in planned expenses may be necessary in order for a consultant to accomplish his/her profit objective.

40. _____ Many independent consultants will find data base programs and spreadsheet programs to be quite useful in their consulting practice.

41. _____ The main problem with computerized accounting programs is that you can't really keep track of your transactions.

42. _____ The only advantage of the internet to an independent consultant is the fact that an appropriate web page can boost his/her consulting practice.

43. _____ It is not good business sense to attempt to insure your consulting business against every conceivable risk.

44. _____ The only advantage that insurance offers the consultant is protection of assets.

45. _____ It is wasteful to purchase liability insurance if you do not have any employees.

46. _____ Theft, robbery, and burglary are different terms for the same phenomenon.

47. _____ It is possible to purchase insurance and so protect yourself from loss due to burglary.

48. _____ Insurance confers limited liability upon single proprietors.

49. _____ Limited partners are not permitted to take part in the management of the firm.

50. _____ By buying insurance, the corporation overcomes the disadvantage of being taxed twice.

ANSWERS

1. F	2. F	3. F	4. T	5. F	6. F	7. F	8. T
9. F	10. T	11. T	12. T	13. F	14. F	15. F	16. F
17. F	18. F	19. T	20. T	21. T	22. F	23. F	24. T
25. T	26. T	27. F	28. T	29. F	30. F	31. F	32. T
33. F	34. F	35. T	36. T	37. F	38. F	39. T	40. T
41. F	42. F	43. T	44. F	45. F	46. F	47. T	48. F
49. T	50. F						

CHAPTER 12
CONSULTING CONTRACTS

INTRODUCTION

Contracts are important in the consulting business. As a matter of fact, some people use the terms "contract" and "assignment" synonymously. For example, a client might say to you, "We have a contract for a business plan. Are you interested?" What the client is actually saying is that an assignment to develop a business plan is available. Of course, assignments and contracts are not identical. An assignment is work that you must perform while a contract is an agreement between you and your client concerning the terms under which you will perform the assignment.

In this chapter, we discuss certain facts that the independent consultant should know about contracts. The more the independent consultant knows about contracts, the less likely it is that he/she will fall pray to breaches of contract, or be done in by contracts. We begin the chapter with a definition of a contract, and in the process, we discuss written and verbal contracts. We then discuss the pros and cons of contracts, after which we outline the contents of a contract and provide an illustration of a simple independent consulting contract. We end the chapter with a discussion of various types of contracts into which an independent consultant might enter.

CONTRACT DEFINED

I am sure that somewhere out there in legal space, there is a proper legal definition of a contract, complete with all the necessary nuances and "legalese" (legal jargon). We noted earlier that the fact that *contracts* and *assignments* are often used synonymously does not make them identical. A contract is not the same thing as an assignment. A contract may be defined as an agreement between two or more *competent* parties for a *legal* purpose and supported by a *consideration*.

At least three things are evident from this definition:

1. The parties to a contract must be competent. This means simply that they must be capable of understanding the agreement into which they are entering. They must be sober (not intoxicated), of sound mind (not insane), and not underage.

2. The agreement must be for a legal purpose. This suggests that an agreement between two people to engage in an illegal activity is an invalid contract. If you enter into an agreement with someone else to pay you $5,000 to steal a diamond ring, you should not expect the courts to enforce such an agreement. Neither should you expect the courts to enforce a contract between you and an arsonist to set fire to your competitor's office.

3. The agreement is supported by a consideration. Presumably, this means that the parties to the agreement have obligations. They promise to do or not to do something. The parties either give up or get something. For example, a carpenter might agree to renovate a basement for a homeowner for a fee of $1,500 (the consideration).

For our purpose at present, we define an independent consulting contract as an agreement between an independent consultant and a client. The consultant agrees to provide certain specified services for the client, and the client agrees to pay for those services as specified in the contract. Two other essentials of a contract are offer and acceptance. We have already discussed consideration. Let us now consider offer and acceptance.

The *offer* is a promise or a proposal. A proposal by an independent consultant to develop a business plan for a client for a fee of $5,000 is an offer. An *acceptance* is simply an agreement to the terms and conditions of an offer. An offer can be withdrawn before acceptance or rejection. If that is the case, the offer is considered expired.

A contract binds the parties to the terms of the agreement for the duration of the contract. Failure to comply with any of the terms by either party constitutes a breach of contract. Before you sign any contract, be sure that you can keep your end of the bargain. A breach of contract on your part may be extremely costly and may do you irreparable damage. A contract should list the terms of the agreement clearly and should spell out, in detail, the obligations of the parties involved.

Written Versus Verbal Contracts

When most people think of a contract, they think of a written document. However, a contract can be either written or verbal.

Verbal Contracts

If a private contractor agrees verbally to build a deck for me for $3,250.00, that agreement constitutes a verbal contract, provided that all the essentials of a contract mentioned above are satisfied. The agreement may be entered into as follows. Let's assume that I visited my brother-in-law last week and saw his new deck which I really admired. I asked him who built his deck and he gave me a business card with the contractor's name and telephone number and volunteered that he paid $3,500.00. Two days later, I called the contractor, and the telephone conversation went like this:

Customer (Me): My name is _____, and I am calling about a deck that I'd like you to build for me.

Contractor: Well, I'll be pleased to build your deck for you, but I won't be able to start on it before Wednesday. Will that be O.K. with you? By the way, who recommend me to you?

Customer: I saw the work you did for my brother-in-law, Dave on 67th Street. He gave me your card. And yes, Wednesday will be fine. How much will it cost?

Contractor: Well, I'll have to come and take the measurements, and I'll give you a figure then. I can do that on Tuesday at about 2:00 p.m. Oh, sorry, make that 2:30. Will that be O.K. with you?

Customer: Yes, That's perfect.

Contractor: What's the address?

Customer: Oh, it's just a few blocks away from Dave's place. We are at 123 Main Street. The telephone number is 123-4567.

The contractor came to my home at 2:30 p.m. on Tuesday. He took the measurements and asked me a few questions about style, waterproofing, and other options that I could have. He sketched what the deck would look like and then did some calculations on a piece of paper. The following dialogue then ensued:

Contractor: Your deck will cost $3,250.00 exactly.

Customer: That's O.K. When will it be finished?

Contractor: Well, I'll start it tomorrow, that's Wednesday, the 16th, and it will be ready by Friday, in the afternoon. You'll have to give me a deposit of $1,000.00, and then you can pay the balance in two monthly installments of $1,125.00 each, starting on the 18th of next month. Is that O.K. with you?

Client: Sure, that's fine. I'll give you the cheque for $1,000.00 right now.

I wrote the cheque for $1,000.00 and handed it to the contractor.

Contractor: Thank you very much. Say hi to Dave when you talk with him again. I'll see you tomorrow morning.

Client: Thank you for coming.

We shook hands and the contractor left. We had an oral contract. There was the offer (his promise to build my deck), the acceptance (I agreed with his proposal and even paid the deposit), and the consideration (I agreed to pay the balance of $2,250.00 in two monthly installments of $1,125.00 each).

If the contractor subsequently tried to get me to pay an extra $200.00, the courts would enforce the oral contract in my favor provided that I could prove that the terms were as outlined above. Therein lies the problem: "If I could prove." Verbal contracts are often difficult to prove, so for that reason, they may not be as good as written contracts. Let us turn now to written contracts.

Written Contracts

Although a great deal of business is still done by "gentlemen's agreements" and "handshakes", most contracts today are not verbal but written. This is hardly surprising since it is often difficult to prove what was agreed to in a verbal contract. A written contract provides documented evidence of precisely what the parties agreed to. Should a dispute arise, the parties can refer to the document and thus usually settle the dispute.

Some of your clients, especially corporate clients, will have their own standard contracts drawn up by their lawyers or their legal departments. There is absolutely nothing wrong with this, provided that you fully understand exactly what the document says, and all its ramifications, before you sign on the dotted line. Written contracts are often shrouded in legal jargon that is totally unintelligible to all except those who are trained in such matters. If a contract is drawn up by your client, have your lawyer read it and explain it to you before you sign it. If you draw up your own contract, have your lawyer review it just to make sure that it does not bind you to anything that is not intended.

Written contracts may be long (hundreds of pages), or they may be short (one or two pages). Most independent consultants are unlikely to have contracts covering several hundreds of pages. On the contrary, their contracts will be no more than two or three pages. If you have control over the contracts that you sign, unless you are a lawyer or someone who is trained in legal terminology, try to ascertain that the document says exactly what the parties agree to in simple terms — that it is drawn up in plain English.

PROS AND CONS OF CONTRACTS

In the remainder of this chapter, our discussion of contracts will refer to written rather than verbal contracts. In this section, we discuss the pros and cons of contracts, beginning with the cons.

The Cons

Contracts place a wedge between consultant and client

Some independent consultants feel that contracts put off their clients, especially if the contracts are lengthy and written in unintelligible legalese rather than in plain simple English. They feel that such contracts serve only to place unnecessary distance between them and their clients.

Contracts introduce an element of mistrust

They feel also that the consultant-client relationship is one of trust and that a contract tends to introduce an element of mistrust. They see the consultant-client relationship as being similar to a doctor-patient relationship. One person needs help and the other can provide it. There is no need for lawyers and contracts in such professional relationships.

Contracts and costly and time-consuming

Opponents of contracts claim, moreover, that contracts are costly and time-consuming since lawyers are often involved in the process of drawing them up or checking and interpreting them.

Contracts reduce your chances of working

According to one well-known independent consultant, trying to get a client to enter into a written contractual agreement cuts the consultant's chances of working in half. He noted that it is the consultant who often tries to get the client to sign a contract, not the other way around. Forcing the client to do something that he/she really does not want to do reduces the consultant's chances of getting an assignment.

Contracts are contrary to independent consulting

Other opponents of contracts claim that a contract marries you, the consultant, to a situation (perhaps an unhappy situation) in which you will be stuck for the duration of the contract. You are stuck because getting out of it constitutes a breach which may prove to be quite costly to you. They view contracts as "entrapments" that are contrary to the very nature of independent consulting — the freedom to be the master of your own destiny. They claim that the consultant-client relationship has a much better chance to thrive in the absence of a contract.

The Pros

We turn now to the pros. We have already touched on some of the advantages of having a written contract. It avoids misunderstandings and it provides documented proof of what has been agreed to.

A contract provides a documented frame of reference

Let us return to the example of the contractor who verbally agreed to build my deck for $3,250 and to complete the job by a certain date. Let us assume that Friday came and the deck is far from finished. I complained to the contractor that he promised to deliver the completed deck on Friday afternoon. He tells me that he meant the following Friday. He also wants me to pay an additional $250.00, claiming that his original quotation was $3,500 and not $3,250. I have no written proof of the agreement that was made. I now have a problem. My deck is not finished and I am asked to pay extra money. If the terms of the agreement were clearly spelled out in a written contract, I would not have that particular problem. The contractor and I could simply refer to the contract and hopefully resolve the conflict. As a last resort, I would have an excellent chance of having the court of law rule in my favor since there would be documented evidence of the agreement.

A contract can help you get paid

Unfortunately, from time to time, you will encounter clients who want you to work but who want you to accept a lower fee than what was agreed to in the contract. Some even try to get away without paying. If you work and don't get paid, you will soon be forced to give up your consulting practice that gives you so much enjoyment. A written contract will help you get paid for your hard but enjoyable work by reminding your clients of their legal obligations to pay the fees stipulated in the contract.

A contract can help keep you out of court

Ironically, one of the purposes of a contract is to protect you if it becomes necessary to go to court, yet one of its roles of the same contract is to keep you from having to go to court. Lawyers are expensive and court costs can be astronomical. In addition, a court case can consume an inordinate amount of precious time. Even if you win a court case, you certainly don't want to have a reputation of being a consultant who takes his/her clients to court. Because it is easier to settle a dispute when a written contract exists than in the absence of one, a written contract can help you stay out of court.

The law requires that some contracts be written

In some jurisdictions, certain transactions require a written contract. These transactions include those having to do with real estate (such as purchases, leases, and rents) and those involving sums over $500.00.

Contracts are necessary in order to get some engagements

Many independent consultants earn a significant part of their income by offering their services to various levels of government and government agencies. These organizations will not engage the services of consultants unless a contract is signed. The consultant then has two options: sign a contract or forget about the assignment.

THE CONTENTS OF A CONTRACT

For lengthy and complicated agreements, it may be necessary to hire a lawyer. If you do draft your own contracts, you could save a good amount of money. Remember to have a lawyer review it before you use it. The legal fees for reviewing a contract are far less than the fees for reviewing a contract. As a general guide, we list here the contents of a simple consulting contract. It is impossible to provide an outline that will be appropriate for all independent consultants or all consulting purposes. What we offer here is the bare minimum that an independent consulting contract should contain.

- The date of the contract
- The names of the parties involved
- The addresses of the parties involved
- An offer (promise)
- An acceptance
- Consideration
- Duration of contract
- Signatures of the parties involved

Illustration 12.1 shows how these essential elements may be blended into a contract.

Illustration 12.1. Example of a Simple Consulting Contract

This contract is made between:

New Age Consulting with offices at 123 Main Street, Any City, Prov., Country, represented by John Henry, hereafter referred to as the **Consultant**

and

ABC Trust Company Ltd. with officers at 67 John Street, Any City, Prov., Country, represented by David Johnson (President and CEO), hereafter referred to as the **Client**.

1. The Consultant offers to provide the following services for the Client:

   A. A comprehensive organizational diagnostic analysis of ABC Trust Co. Ltd.

   B. Produce two bound copies of the report of the analysis to the Client.

2. The Consultant shall begin the work on June 26, 2024 and complete it no later than July 24, 2024.

3. The Client will pay the Consultant $15,000 for the performance of this assignment, one half ($7,500) payable upon the signing of this agreement, and the remaining $7,500 payable upon delivery of the report

4. The Client agrees to pay the consultant interest at the rate of _____percent per year on any overdue payments under the terms of this contract.

5. The terms of this agreement cannot be amended unless such amendment is agreed to in writing and signed by both parties.

6. This agreement is governed by the laws of _____.

Signed:

_____

for ABC Trust Co. Ltd.

_____

for New Age Consulting

Date_____

     Day   Month   Year

Let us analyze the above contract carefully. The contract begins with an identification of the parties (New Age Consulting and ABC Trust Co. Ltd.). Their addresses are also included.

Paragraph 1 of the contract takes care of the *offer (promise).* "The Consultant offers to provide the following services ...", and the services are listed specifically.

The *time* element (duration) is handled in paragraph 2. The beginning and completion dates are specified. The contract takes effect on June 26, 2024, and terminates on July 24, 2024.

Paragraph 3 takes care of the *consideration*. The services will be provided for a fee of $15,000, and the payment terms are clearly indicated.

Paragraph 4 specifies the consequence of not settling the account by the due date, while paragraph 5 sets forth the conditions for amending the contract.

Paragraph 6 indicates the jurisdiction that governs the agreement.
The signature of the client at the end of the contract signifies *acceptance*, and the *date* appears at the end.

ALTERNATIVES TO CONTRACTS

For those independent consultants who are uneasy or uncomfortable about the idea of trying to force their clients and prospective clients into signing intimidating contracts, or who may still not be convinced that contracts are necessary, I have two very simple, yet sensible, alternatives:

1. 1, A letter of engagement

2. An authorization to proceed.

Let us deal with each of these two alternatives in turn, starting with the letter of engagement.

Letter of Engagement

A letter of engagement is a written confirmation that the client agrees to engage the services of the consultant to perform a certain function for a specified fee. The letter of engagement contains essentially the same information as a formal written contract, but it is much less complex and often does not require the services of a lawyer. An example of a letter of engagement is presented as Illustration 12.2. It is certainly less intimidating and therefore more palatable than the normal formal written contract.

Note the following points about the letter of engagement.

- It states your understanding of the terms of the engagement.

- It provides an opportunity for the client to register any disagreement with your understanding of those terms.

- Its friendly tone is probably more in tune with the consultant-client relationship than may be the case with a written formal contract.

- The client's signature serves as confirmation that your understanding of the terms of the agreement is the same as the client's.

I have used letters of engagement on numerous occasions, and I have found that clients hardly ever object to their use. After all, it's only a letter. Right? But just in case there is a dispute about the assignment or the cost, that letter of engagement will stand up in any court of law.

Illustration 12.2. Example of a Letter of Engagement

June 15, 2024

Mr. David Johnson, President
ABC Trust Co. Ltd.
67 John Street
Any City, Prov.
Country.

I thoroughly enjoyed our luncheon meeting today and our discussion about operations at ABC Trust Co. Ltd. I share your view that a thorough diagnostic analysis is necessary.

The main purpose of this letter is to confirm the agreement for New Age Consulting to conduct a comprehensive organizational diagnostic analysis of operations at ABC Trust Co.

As agreed, we will begin the work on June 26, 2024, and complete it by July 24, 2024. The cost will be $15,000, one-half payable upon your signing this letter, and the balance payable upon delivery of two bound copies of the report on the assignment.

This is an exciting project, David, and I am sure that we will enjoy working on it with you as we have enjoyed working on other projects for ABC Trust Co. Of course, you may call me at any time if you have any questions.

Please indicate your agreement to the above terms by signing below as indicated, and returning a copy of the letter to me as soon as possible.

Sincerely,
John Henry
Consultant

Engagement Agreement

I hereby confirm the agreement for New Age to perform the assignment under the terms mentioned above.

David Johnson
ABC Trust Co. Ltd.

Authorization to Proceed

We turn now to the authorization to proceed. This is actually a very skillful device to convert a proposal into a contract. Once the proposal is accepted, the authorization to proceed simply gives you, the consultant, the permission to proceed with the assignment according to the terms outlined in the proposal. It may consist of only one or two sentences.

In Chapter 7, we showed how, by using an authorization to proceed, the consultant can turn a proposal into a contract. The authorization to proceed appears at the end of the proposal and may be stated in terms such as:

Authorization to Proceed

I/We have read the proposal pertaining to ----------------, and authorize New Age Consulting to proceed with the assignment according to the terms outlined in the proposal.

_____ Date_____

David Johnson   Day   Month   Year

ABC Trust Co. Ltd.

Note that the Authorization to Proceed should be signed and dated.

TYPES OF CONTRACTS

Contracts can be classified in a variety of ways. However, the types of contracts that the independent consultant is likely to encounter may be classified according to the method of fee-setting used by the independent consultant. Under this classification system, we can identify and discuss the following types of contracts:

> Time/cost contracts
> Performance-based contracts
> Fixed-fee contracts
> Retainer-based contracts

We shall discuss each of these types of contracts in turn. Of course, hybrid versions of the above types of contracts are also quite common. For example, a contract could be drawn up with both fixed fee and time/cost elements. Such a contract could specify that your costs will be paid plus a predetermined (fixed) amount for your time.

Time/Cost Contracts

Time/Cost contracts are akin to billing on an hourly or daily basis. Under such a contract, you are paid on the basis of the amount of time spent on the assignment and according to the expenses incurred. For obvious reasons, independent consultants tend to favor this type of contract. It's simple. You do the work and you are paid.

Many clients oppose time/cost contracts, fearing that some unscrupulous consultants will deliberately prolong assignments to increase their incomes. You may be able to surmount this mistrust by placing an upper limit on your fee. The contract could include a clause such as: "The fee for this assignment will not exceed $6,000.00." If you can bring in the assignment at less than $6,000.00, it will increase your client's faith in you.

Performance-Based Contracts

This type of contract is analogous to billing on a performance basis. A performance-based contract ties your fee to your performance. These types of contracts are not nearly as popular as time/cost contracts among independent consultants. However, for some types of consulting, performance contracts may be appropriate. For example, recruiting consultants may be paid based on the number of employees they can place. You should be wary of performance-based contracts unless you are quite sure that you can deliver the goods. In Chapter 6, we indicated cases where performance-based contracts may be advantageous to the independent consultant.

Fixed-Fee Contracts

Fixed-fee contracts are clearly related to billing on a fixed-fee basis. Under such a contract, you are paid a fixed amount for the assignment, whether you complete it in a day or a week.   If you enter into a fixed-fee contract, you must be careful to estimate the work properly. Quite often, it is extremely difficult to visualize the problems that you may encounter when trying to find a solution to your client's problem. You have no way of knowing how much time the assignment will actually take. In such cases, it is probably good advice to eschew fixed-fee contracts.

Retainer-Based Contracts

Once you have established a good relationship with your clients and have won their confidence, you may be able to provide consulting services to them under the terms of a retainer-based contract. Under such a contract, you receive a constant monthly fee in exchange for the insurance of a certain amount of your time, whether or not the time is actually used.   Many independent consultants who have proved their worth enjoy the benefits of a retainer-based contract.   The contract guarantees you a monthly income.   Clients feel comfortable entering into such an agreement because it gives them quick access to your expert advice whenever they need it.

CHAPTER SUMMARY

1. A contract may be defined as an agreement between two or more competent parties for a legal purpose and supported by a consideration.

2. The essentials of a contract are an offer (promise), acceptance, and consideration.

3. Contracts may be verbal or written.   Written contracts are more easily enforced than verbal

contracts, because, in the case of a verbal contract, it is often difficult to prove what was said.

4. Written contracts may be long or short. Before you sign a contract, you should make sure that you understand its terms and conditions. The services of a lawyer may be required.

5. Opponents of formal written contracts claim that they adversely affect the consultant-client relationship. Proponents, on the other hand, claim that written contracts protect the independent consultant in many ways.

6. A contract should contain the date of the agreement, the identities of the parties involved, the offer, the acceptance, the consideration, the duration of the agreement, and the signatures of the parties.

7. Letters of engagement and authorization to proceed are alternatives to formal contracts.

8. Types of contracts include time/cost contracts, performance-based contracts, fixed-fee contracts, and retainer-based contracts.

SELF-TEST QUESTIONS

Indicate whether each of the following is true (T) or false (F).

1. _____ As long as you sign an agreement, it becomes an enforceable contract.

2. _____ Once an offer is made in a contract, it can never be withdrawn.

3. _____ Essential elements of a contract are an offer, an acceptance, and a consideration.

4. _____ In order for a contract to be valid, it has to be written, signed, and dated.

5. _____ Oral contracts are legally binding provided that the terms of the agreement can be substantiated.

6. _____ On no account should an independent consultant accept an assignment without a written contract.

7. _____ Opponents of formal written contracts claim that such contracts reduce your chances of working substantially.

8. _____ It is generally accepted by the independent consulting profession that formal written contracts do more harm than good.

9. _____ In some jurisdictions, certain types of transactions require written contracts.

10. _____ A written contract can help to keep you out of court and can help you get paid.

11. _____ As a bare minimum, an independent consulting contract should contain the identities of the parties, an offer, a consideration, an acceptance, the duration of the agreement, the date, and the signatures of the parties.

12. _____ Consultants have the option of using a contract or not using one. There are no other alternatives.

13. _____ A letter of engagement is a written confirmation that the client agrees to engage the services of the consultant to perform a certain function for a specified fee.

14. _____ Clients almost always object to the use of letters of engagement because they lack the force of contracts.

15. _____ The main advantage of a contract over a letter of engagement is that the letter of engagement cannot be enforced by a court of law.

16. _____ A proposal is a proposal, and there is no way to convert it into a contract.

17. _____ An authorization to proceed with an assignment is more palatable and less intimidating than a formal contract.

18. _____ Time/cost contracts are identical to fixed-fee contracts.

19. _____ Clients tend to oppose time/cost contracts because of the possibility that consultants may prolong assignments unduly, just to increase their income.

20. _____ Performance-based contracts can never be advantageous to individual consultants. They should therefore be avoided at all cost.

21. _____ Under a fixed-fee contract, you are paid a fixed amount for an assignment regardless of the time it takes to complete the assignment.

22. _____ One of the great advantages of a retainer-based contract is that it provides you with a guaranteed monthly income.

ANSWERS

1. F   2. F   3. T   4. F   5. T   6. F   7. T   8. F

9. T   10. T   11. T   12. F   13. T   14. F   15. F   16. F

17. T   18. F   19. T   20. F   21. T   22. T

CHAPTER 13
INDEPENDENT CONSULTING AND ARTIFICIAL INTELLIGENCE

INTRODUCTION

In today's rapidly evolving business landscape, Artificial Intelligence (AI) has emerged as a transformative force across industries. For independent consultants, embracing AI is no longer optional—it's a strategic necessity. This chapter explores how independent consultants can leverage AI to enhance their services, streamline operations, and deliver greater value to their clients. By understanding AI's potential and practical applications, consultants can stay competitive in an increasingly tech-driven world.

DEFINITION OF ARTIFICIAL INTELLIGENCE (AI)

Artificial Intelligence refers to the simulation of human intelligence by machines programmed to think, learn, and make decisions. AI encompasses a wide range of technologies, including:

- *Machine Learning (ML):* Algorithms that enable systems to learn and improve from experience.

- *Natural Language Processing (NLP):* Tools like chatbots and virtual assistants that interpret and respond to human language.

- *Predictive Analytics:* Systems that analyze data to forecast trends and outcomes.

- *Automation Tools:* Software that performs repetitive tasks with minimal human intervention.

For independent consultants, AI provides opportunities to enhance problem-solving capabilities and optimize client outcomes.

USING AI IN INDEPENDENT CONSULTING

1. Enhancing Data Analysis

AI tools can process and analyze vast amounts of data quickly and accurately. Among other things, consultants can use AI to:

- Identify patterns and trends.
- Provide data-driven recommendations.
- Generate insights that add value to client projects.

2. Automating Routine Tasks

AI-powered automation tools can handle time-consuming tasks such as:

- Scheduling meetings.
- Managing emails.
- Generating reports.

By automating these processes, consultants can focus on high-value strategic work.

3. Customizing Client Solutions

AI enables consultants to tailor services to individual client needs by:

- Using predictive analytics to forecast outcomes.
- Developing personalized strategies based on client-specific data.
- Building scalable models that adapt to client growth.

4. Improving Client Communication

Natural Language Processing (NLP) tools can enhance communication by:

- Automating responses to frequently asked questions.
- Creating clear, data-backed presentations.
- Facilitating real-time language translation for global clients.

5. Staying Ahead of Industry Trends

AI tools like sentiment analysis and market trend forecasting help consultants stay informed about industry developments. This foresight allows consultants to proactively advise clients and position themselves as thought leaders.

6. Ethical Considerations

While using AI, consultants must ensure:

- **Transparency:** Clearly communicate how AI is used in projects.

- **Data Privacy:** Protect client data with robust security measures.
- **Bias Mitigation:** Monitor AI algorithms to prevent discriminatory outcomes.

CHAPTER SUMMARY

1. Artificial Intelligence (AI) is a set of technologies that enable computers to perform a variety of advanced functions, including the ability to understand and translate spoken and written language, analyze data, make recommendations, and more.

2. AI is revolutionizing the consulting industry, providing tools to enhance efficiency, deepen insights, and deliver exceptional value to clients.

3. By integrating AI into their practices, independent consultants can stay competitive and future-ready.

4. However, success with AI requires continuous learning, ethical application, and a commitment to aligning technology with client needs.

SELF-TEST QUESTIONS

Indicate whether each of the following is true (T) or false (F).

1._____ Artificial Intelligence is primarily concerned with simulating human intelligence in machines.

2._____ Machine Learning is a subset of AI that focuses on automating repetitive tasks without requiring human input.

3._____ Independent consultants can use AI tools to identify patterns and trends in client data.

4._____ Predictive analytics is used by consultants to forecast future trends based on historical data.

5._____ AI tools cannot enhance client communication because they lack emotional understanding.

6._____ Automating routine tasks through AI allows consultants to focus more on strategic activities.

7._____ Sentiment analysis is a technique within AI that helps consultants monitor industry trends.

8._____ Using AI in consulting guarantees ethical outcomes without additional oversight.

9._____ Natural Language Processing is an AI technology that enables tools like chatbots to interact with human language.

10._____ AI cannot help consultants who work in industries with complex and unstructured data.

11._____ Consultants should prioritize transparency when integrating AI into client projects.

12._____ Data privacy concerns are a minor issue when using AI in consulting.

13._____ Bias in AI algorithms can be mitigated by proper monitoring and diverse data sets.

14._____ AI allows consultants to scale their operations without sacrificing quality.

15._____ Consultants using AI tools must still apply their expertise to contextualize insights and recommendations.

ANSWERS

1. T   2. F   3. T   4. T   5. F   6. T   7. T   8. F

9. T   10. F   11. T   12. F   13. T   14. T   15. T

CHAPTER 14
THE FUTURE OF
INDEPENDENT CONSULTING

INTRODUCTION

The landscape of independent consulting is evolving rapidly, driven by technological advancements, global economic shifts, and changing client expectations. Consultants must adapt to these changes to stay relevant and competitive. This chapter explores key trends shaping the future of independent consulting, strategies for navigating emerging challenges, and opportunities to thrive in a dynamic marketplace.

KEY TRENDS SHAPING THE FUTURE OF CONSULTING

Increased Client Expectations

Clients now demand more than traditional expertise; they expect innovative, data-driven solutions and measurable outcomes.

- Consultants must integrate advanced tools and methodologies into their services.

- Offering customized, actionable insights will set consultants apart in a crowded marketplace.

Digital Transformation

The rise of digital technologies is reshaping how consulting services are delivered.

- Virtual consultations, digital platforms, and online workshops are becoming standard.
- Consultants must adapt to hybrid work environments and leverage digital tools for collaboration.

The Globalization of Consulting

Remote work and virtual communication have made it easier for consultants to access clients worldwide.

- Cross-border projects and multicultural client interactions are becoming common.
- Understanding global business dynamics is increasingly essential.

Emphasis on Sustainability and Ethics

Clients are prioritizing sustainability and ethical practices, seeking consultants who align with these values.

- Consultants can position themselves as leaders in sustainable and socially responsible practices.

CHALLENGES FACING INDEPENDENT CONSULTANTS

Competition from Larger Firms

Big firms are leveraging AI and other technologies to offer faster, cheaper services, creating challenges for independent consultants.

- Independent consultants must emphasize personalized service and niche expertise to compete.

Staying Current with Technology

The rapid pace of technological change can be overwhelming.

- Continuous learning is critical to mastering tools like AI, data analytics, and automation platforms.

Navigating Regulatory Changes

Consultants working globally face differing legal, tax, and compliance requirements.

- Staying informed about regulations in various markets will minimize risk and enhance service offerings.

OPPORTUNITIES FOR GROWTH

Specialization in Niche Markets

As industries become more complex, clients seek experts with in-depth knowledge of specific fields.

- Consultants can differentiate themselves by targeting niche markets and industries.

Leveraging Technology for Scalability

AI, automation, and digital platforms allow consultants to expand their reach and serve more clients without compromising quality.

- Creating digital products, such as eBooks or online courses, offers an additional revenue stream.

Building Collaborative Networks

Partnering with other consultants or firms can open doors to larger projects and diverse expertise.

- Collaborative networks also provide access to shared resources and new client bases.

Becoming a Thought Leader

Publishing articles, hosting webinars, and speaking at industry events can position consultants as trusted authorities in their field.

- Building a strong personal brand ensures long-term success and credibility.

CHAPTER SUMMARY

1. The consultant's world of work is changing rapidly because of technological change.

2. The future of independent consulting is filled with opportunities and challenges.

3. By staying adaptable, embracing technology, and focusing on delivering exceptional value, consultants can thrive in a dynamic and competitive environment.

4. The key to success lies in continuous learning, fostering relationships, and leveraging emerging trends to meet evolving client needs.

SELF-TEST QUESTIONS

Indicate whether each of the following is true (T) or false (F).

1. _____ Independent consulting is immune to changes in client expectations.

2. _____ Digital transformation is reshaping the way consulting services are delivered.

3. _____ Consultants who focus on sustainability and ethics can attract more clients.

4. _____ Competing with larger firms requires independent consultants to lower their rates.

5. _____ Cross-border consulting requires awareness of global business dynamics.

6. _____ Continuous learning is essential for staying competitive in the consulting industry.

7. _____ Consultants can leverage AI and automation to scale their services effectively.

8. _____ Niche specialization is becoming less relevant in a global consulting market.

9. _____ Building collaborative networks can help consultants access larger projects.

10. _____ Thought leadership has no impact on a consultant's credibility.

11. _____ The future of consulting is entirely driven by technology, with no focus on ethics or sustainability.

12. _____ Personalization and niche expertise are key differentiators for independent consultants.

13. _____ Offering digital products like eBooks or courses is a way to diversify income streams.

14. _____ Regulatory changes are irrelevant for consultants working locally.

15. _____ Independent consultants must embrace adaptability to succeed in the future.

ANSWERS

1. F   2. T   3. T   4. F   5. T   6. T   7. T   8. F

9. T   10. F   11. F   12. T   13. T   14. F   15. T